Maverick Navy

Ensign Moffat, New York, June 1917

Maverick Navy

by

Alexander W. Moffat,
Captain, USNR (Ret.)

Wesleyan University Press
Middletown, Connecticut

Library of Congress Cataloging in Publication Data

Moffat, Alexander White, 1891–
    Maverick Navy

    1. European War, 1914–1918—Naval operations—
Submarine. 2. European War, 1914–1918—Naval
operations, American. 3. European War, 1914–1918—
Personal narratives, American. 4. Moffat, Alexander
White, 1891–   I. Title.
D595.A45M63   940.4 ′513′73   76–7191
ISBN 0–8195–5000–0

Book design by Jorgen G. Hansen
Manufactured in the United States of America
First Edition

Contents

List of Illustrations

Maverick Navy

Preface

ALTHOUGH I had the privilege of serving six years of active duty in World War II, it is World War I that provides the background for this haphazard record of experiences, many unorthodox, which I encountered as an untrained amateur commissioned officer.

My first assignment as a lowly ensign was to command a converted yacht. This was unfortunate since, by Navy standards, command afloat is starting at the top, whatever the commander's rank. The Navy assumed training and experience to which I had not been exposed. I consider this a mistake on the part of the Navy. It was the first of many mistakes, some the Navy's, some mine, despite which the job usually got done.

This is definitely not a war book. It deals with a reserve officer's progression from civilian ignorance to a professionalism of sorts based on his learning to interpret naval regulations to serve the best interests of the job at hand.

Certainly this metamorphasis could not have occurred without the patient self-control of several Naval Academy graduates under whom I served. Often a superior closed one eye to help me stay out of trouble. Of this I was at the time aware, but usually only fully appreciated after the fact.

Some names in this book are true, others fictitious. I have used fictitious names only in two circumstances:

(a) When my memory has let me down and no source is readily available for looking up the real name.

(b) When an individual must be presented in an unflattering light, which might distress his surviving family.

ALEXANDER W. MOFFAT

Manchester, Massachusetts
February, 1976

Chapter 1

Tamarack, S.P. 561, *New York*

ON JUNE 15, 1917, USS *Tamarack, S.P. 561*, presumably in all respects ready for sea, proceeded from Nevins' Yard at City Island, New York, where she had been converted to naval service, to the Section Base in Gravesend Bay in lower New York harbor where she reported for duty.

Tamarack was a beautiful eighty-foot yacht, twin-screw, with a cruising speed of sixteen knots. She had been capably handled by a crew of three: captain, engineer, and steward. In her incarnation the Navy had entrusted her to a crew of one officer and nine enlisted men, all reserves with little or no Navy training.

I, a newly created ensign with experience only in small sailing yachts in coastwise cruising, was in command. Below decks Chief Machinist's Mate Fernald, fortunately in civilian life head service man for the firm that had built *Tamarack*'s engines, had the machinery under complete control. His gifted preventive maintenance was to win for *Tamarack* a reputation for reliable operation unequalled in the Section Patrol fleet.

The only man aboard with any Navy background was my red-headed brother-in-law, Ted DeCamp. On graduating from Harvard he had joined the Naval Reserve as apprentice seaman, finished boot camp training, and had been assigned to the battleship *Virginia*. In ten months he had progressed to signal quartermaster third class. I managed to get him transferred to *Tamarack*.

Our electrician third class for radio was an accomplished ham radio operator who could double on the signal lamp. He was an incredibly ingenuous youth whom the crew delighted always in addressing by his full name, Philander Hammer Betts.

The other six crew members were rated seamen. The cook was a barber from New Rochelle who worked at night as a hash slinger in a lunch wagon. Griswold was a trainee in public utilities. Ketchum worked in a brokerage office; little Ablowich was a salesman from the Bronx. Wright was a wealthy playboy friend of the owner, Len Breed. Breed, who was two classes ahead of me at Harvard, had bought *Tamarack* to lease to the Navy for a dollar a year so he could ship aboard. Wright and Breed had never taken an order in their lives. My two problem children.

This, then, was the motley ship's company that tied up in Marine Basin that hot June afternoon. I reported *Tamarack*'s arrival to the duty officer and was directed to the supply office to make arrangements about provisioning. The next morning I was to report to the base commander at 0900 hours for orders.

In retrospect, the last eight weeks had been the most exacting and unpredictable of my life, beginning with the moment on the 5:25 train to Flushing when Len Breed made room for me beside him.

He was our most talked of neighbor, a ruthless, irrepressible live wire who had been lucky so many times that success had become a habit. He had made money, married money, and made still more money, wearing as an armor the conviction that he could not fail. Men envied his achievements but, save for a few sycophants, accepted him with reservations. I had known him slightly in college and had found in him some qualities to like, if few to admire.

It came as somewhat of a surprise to hear that he contemplated enlisting in the Navy. Always direct in method, he made a suggestion that, coming from anyone else, would have sounded ridiculous.

"I've got the dope." Len always had the dope. "The thing to do is lease your yacht to the Navy at a dollar a year and ship on it with a bunch of good fellows as crew. Then you sail around New York harbor all day and go ashore every night."

That was not my idea of the national emergency. "That may be the dope, but I don't believe the Navy can use my small auxiliary yawl, and unless you've been keeping it quiet, you don't own a yacht."

"Of course I don't," he replied impatiently, "but we can buy one, can't we?"

"Where do you get this 'we' stuff?" I said. It's all I can do to support a wife and two children, much less buy the kind of yacht the Navy wants."

"What kind is that?"

"Big steam yachts or high speed motor cruisers suitable for patrol work," I hazarded.

"How much do they cost — I mean one of these motor cruisers — a snappy one?"

"Anywhere from ten to a hundred thousand dollars."

"Could you get a good one for say, $35,000?" he asked quickly.

"Probably."

"Good. You see what you can buy for $35,000 and then we'll get a couple of friends of mine and enlist on it. I'll tell them you are to be captain. Can you buy the boat tomorrow?"

"Wait a minute, Len. This afternoon I passed an examination for machinist's mate. Tomorrow I've got to take the physical and sign up."

"Don't do it. Get the yacht first. Then we'll find out what rating you have to hold to be captain and then you sign up as that."

The proposition was both dazing and fantastic.

"Listen, Len," I said anxiously, "I've never handled an express cruiser. I may be able to find my way coastwise with a little yawl but that's a long way from handling a big power boat Navy fashion."

"You know more about it than half the men who are going in," he retorted. "Anyway, we'll do it. I'll take a chance if you will. Call me at the office tomorrow as soon as you find the right yacht."

That evening I reported the day's events to Sally. A remark she made across the table haunted me many times in the succeeding months. "You are going to have your hands full if you undertake responsibility for the actions of Leonard Breed and his friends."

Subsequently, I learned to pay more heed to these omniscient warnings of Sally's.

The next morning, instead of reporting for my physical, I repaired to a leading yacht brokerage firm in downtown New York, where I examined the plans and specifications of yachts on the Navy's inspected and approved list that came within Len's price limit.

I agreed to buy *Tamarack*, an eighty-foot twin screw express cruiser, contacted Len, took his check to the bank for certification, paid the broker in exchange for a clear bill of sale, and then had him draw up a form of lease of the vessel from Leonard Breed to the United States Navy for one dollar per year.

I met Len at headquarters of the Third Naval District at the Navy Yard, produced plans, specifications, and photographs of *Tamarack*, and passed papers. The quartet of high ranking officers acting for the commandant agreed to Len's conditions about crew, subject to confirmation by the Bureau of Navigation.

I ascertained the name of the district personnel officer, Lieutenant Commander Starr Taintor, USN, with offices at 280 Broadway in New York City.

It was too late by that time to call on him. This had been a whirlwind day. I went home to report to Sally and to share with her a much needed cocktail before dinner.

The next morning at nine o'clock I was at the personnel office. After a long wait, I was ushered into a small office, courteously greeted by Commander Taintor, a trim, middle-aged man in shirt sleeves sitting at a desk piled high with folders. He held my card, which told him I was vice president of the Transport Tractor Company of Long Island City.

"What can I do for you, Mr. Moffat?" He waved me to a chair.

"I come for advice, sir. I'll be as brief as possible with a rather incredible story."

When I had finished recounting my activities from the time I entered the recruiting office until the *Tamarack* was accepted for naval service, Commander Taintor grinned.

"This war has produced some wacky situations, but this is the wackiest I've come across. You certainly have had a busy forty-eight hours.

"Now suppose you tell me about your background and experience afloat. Until I hear from the bureau I'll stick my neck out for the umpteenth time and set up an arbitrary complement. I'll assume that eighty feet will require a chief petty officer in charge."

When I had finished, he said, "Do you think you can pass a brief oral examination for chief boatswain's mate?"

"I don't know, sir, but I'd like to try."

He said to a yeoman who answered his buzzer, "Send in Chief Bacon.

An elderly chief quartermaster with gold service stripes up to his elbow appeared.

The Commander said, "Bacon, this is Mr. Moffat. He has had quite a bit of experience in small craft. Forget about battlewagons for the moment and find out if he knows enough about piloting and seamanship to handle an eighty-foot yacht. If you say okay, I shall order him as chief boatswain's mate in charge to a yacht just taken over by the Navy. And don't expect him to know anything whatever about the Navy. He'll learn that the hard way."

"Aye, aye, sir. I understand. Come with me."

"When you are through with him, report back to me. I'll have an order ready for you to take him to his physical."

That is how I entered the United States Naval Reserve as a provisional chief boatswain's mate, fourth class.

Sally took the news as I knew she would, without recrimination, just an extra hug. "You'll be doing just what you love to do, mess around boats. The children and I will get along just fine — somehow."

At Nevins' Yard, City Island, the next morning, I inquired for the *Tamarack*. She was hauled out on the ways and looked so vast that I could only stare in consternation at what I had let myself in for. Climbing a tall ladder to the deck I found on board the yacht captain in whose charge she had been since she was built. He had packed his gear and was about to depart, but obligingly remained to inspect every part of the ship and inventory with me.

Nobody seemed to be interested in the *Tamarack* or me or to be able to furnish the kind of information I sought. Then I ran across George Atwood, in command of the *Rutoma*, a yacht being converted in Jacobs' Yard, next door. He had graduated as a lieutenant, junior grade, from the ninety-day course for reserve officers at Annapolis. From him I gleaned a few pointers, among them that I should obtain a copy of Navy regulations and that I was not expected to stay aboard my ship all the time. I liked George immediately, his hard blue eyes, his crisp speech and his vigor. We became close friends. We were the same age, both married, and each had two children. A year later, I owed my ship and my life to his daring seamanship. We never expected our paths to cross as they did.

On May 31 an enlisted man from the personnel office located me in *Tamarack*'s beautiful white enameled engine room. He said he was to transport me downtown in his side car; I was to report to Commander Taintor. No, he didn't know why. This was my first communication from headquarters since being enrolled as a chief boatswain's mate.

On the ride I tried to figure where I had slipped up, but was too distracted by the hazards of a side car driven in traffic by an emancipated cowboy to come up with an answer.

I presented myself at Commander Taintor's desk, hoping I didn't look as nervous as I felt. "You sent for me, sir?"

"Yes, I did. Good morning, Moffat. It seems I made a mistake." My heart sank. "When you were sworn in as a chief boatswain's mate it was my intention to assign you to the *Tamarack* as petty officer in charge." He rummaged in a desk basket. "It has been politely called to my attention by higher authority that I made a mistake. *Tamarack* must be commanded by a commissioned officer." He found the letter he sought. "If you were an ensign it would be within my authority to assign you to this appointment. Have you any objection to being an ensign?"

I was aghast. "No, sir, but I have no training whatever to be an officer."

He said, drily, "Bacon seemed to think you were capable of handling the *Tamarack* as a chief boatswain's mate. I don't see why you would not be equally capable as an ensign. Here, read this."

The letter he proffered was from the Office of the Commandant, addressed to Alex. W. Moffat, CBM. Subject: Provisional appointment of CBM Alex. W. Moffat, USNRF (class 4) terminated. The single paragraph read, in typical Navy lingo:

1. In view of the fact that you will be given a provisional appointment as Ensign from and including June 1, 1917, your enrollment as CBM is hereby terminated from and including May 31, 1917, and the Disbursing Officer, Third Naval District, has been directed to close out your accounts as CBM as of and including May 31, 1917.

Commander Taintor was smiling, probably at the expression on my face. "If you have no objection, Mr. Moffat, I shall have you sworn in, here and now. It will save time, in spite of the commandant's authorization being dated tomorrow." He pushed a call button, "Send in the enrolling officer."

There appeared a very young ensign fully uniformed, including cap. He had shiny pink cheeks, a shiny gold stripe, and shiny shoes. He also wore gloves and a sword.

The oath of office solemnly executed, he disappeared.

Commander Taintor smiled. "Your pay accounts are being taken up by the disbursing officer. The orderly is standing by to return you to City Island. Tomorrow I suggest you get yourself fitted out. Stop in here to pick up your orders. You can then look over the list of available enlisted personnel for *Tamarack*. He grinned, "In addition to your two problem seamen, that is. No crew will be ordered until your ship is ready for commissioning. Good luck to you." He rose and held out his hand.

Then home to report.

At the door I was met by our daughter Mari and the bull terrier who entwined themselves around my legs. Sally was engaged upstairs with the baby. She called down, "Surprise, surprise! Here's Ted."

Ted, smiling, came down the stairs, wearing on his sleeve the insignia of a quartermaster third class. With so many unanswered questions in my mind, I could not have been gladder to see anybody. He was the answer to a prayer.

"Good to see you, Ted. Congratulations on your rating. Where is your battlewagon now?"

"Still in the Boston Navy Yard for an extensive overhaul. Things are quiet in my department, so I grabbed some leave to come down and catch up with you and Sal and the kids."

When Sally came down, Lizzie Burke in the kitchen produced ice and glasses. I broke my news. That was a long evening. As Ted held forth on the Navy and its ways, I was more than ever convinced that I must find somebody to guide me through the labyrinth I had entered. It was then that I had a bright idea.

"Look, Ted, the crew has not yet been picked for *Tamarack*. If you would like to serve with me, I'll see if I can arrange a transfer. I haven't an idea how these things are done, but I am to see Commander Taintor tomorrow to arrange about crew. We sure will need a signalman. Maybe you feel it would be a comedown, but what do you say?"

"It will be the neatest trick of the week if you can do it. I say yes. Being number one on a patrol boat is better than being tenth in line on a battleship."

I don't know how it was accomplished, but within a week Ted reported, with seabag and orders, duly transferred to *Tamarack*.

By June 13 most of the yard work had been completed. *Tamarack* was launched and lay at the pier. I had run all machinery to check that the engines were in good operating condition, but we had not yet been under way. The very next day a lieutenant named Ayers, accompanied by an ensign and two machinist's mates, came on board to run engine-room trials.

I asked Ayers if he accepted responsibility for the ship during the proposed trip, or whether he wished me to take it. He said he was in command of the vessel because he was in command of the trial-trip crew, but that I was responsible because I was in charge. These sounded like weasel words to me. I told him firmly that we would not cast off until the responsibility for the movements of the vessel was definitely assumed by him or by me, that the responsibility could not be divided. He backed down and agreed to accept the responsibility for the vessel, so I wrote a paragraph to that effect in the ship's log and made him sign it. This was a first hunch about covering tracks in the Navy, but it taught me a lesson.

He ran *Tamarack* aground, fortunately on mud bottom with a flooding tide. My paragraph in the log saved me. It transpired that this was his third offense in grounding vessels on trial runs.

This was, of course, the first time I had handled *Tamarack* under way. She responded like a dream. Over a measured mile wide open with no vibration, she clocked 17.5 knots. Mechanically, it was a perfect score. On departing, the lieutenant murmured, "Wish they were all like this one."

The morning of June 14 my orders arrived, via my friend the mail orderly and his side car.

Things were still moving fast. The next morning a phone call from a lieutenant at the Navy Yard, whose name I did not catch, directed that the *Tamarack*, having completed machinery trials, proceed to a berth at the yard to be placed in commission. On arrival I was to report to his office in Building No. 1. On completion of commissioning, *Tamarack* would return to City Island to await orders. He described where I was to tie up and gave the number of his room in Building No. 1. He hung up without giving me a chance to explain that the crew had not appeared.

"Good thing we have engine controls at the wheel," said Ted, when I told him we were getting under way, "And by the way, we only have a yacht ensign so I bought us a United States flag when I was off duty yesterday. We have to hoist it at the commissioning."

"Thanks. I'll square it with you later. You go up to the office and tell them to save this berth for us. I don't know how long it takes to sprinkle the holy water, or whatever they do, but tell them we expect to be back this afternoon."

Big as *Tamarack* seemed to us, her former skipper told me that she had always been operated by him and one hand, with an assist from the steward when necessary. I was an experienced engine man, Ted a competent helmsman, the weather was fine, and we had the appropriate chart. To this day, I don't understand why our trip to the Navy Yard stirred up such a hornet's nest.

The passage down the East River through Hell Gate was uneventful except for dodging tugs and barges. The engines purred like kittens.

At Building No. 1, I located the lieutenant who had phoned. A dozen letter trays on his desk were overflowing with papers. He was hot and harried, a sallow, humorless-looking man who probably had the disposition of a sick wasp. Briefly acknowledging my presence, he said, "Go back aboard and muster your crew. Uniform of the day is whites, and I mean white whites not dirty whites. I'll be aboard in ten minutes."

I saluted, said, "Yes, sir," and left him trying to find papers.

Ted had bent the new United States ensign to the halyards on the staff at the stern ready for hoisting. He and I were at the rail when the lieutenant came aboard.

"I thought I told you to have the crew at muster," he roared. "Rout them out and call them to attention. I haven't got all day!"

One of the few things I had so far learned in the Navy was to stand straight, with my heels together, when in the presence of an officer, and never forget the "sir." I barked at Ted who was three feet away, "Crew. Atten*shun!*" Then I saluted and said to the lieutenant, "The crew is at attention, sir."

"Don't try to be funny with me. Rout 'em out."

"This is all the crew that has been sent to me, sir."

"Who brought the ship from City Island, then?"

"We did, sir. Those were your orders."

The lieutenant contained himself with difficulty. Finally he shook his head. "I'll be everlastingly damned," he said. "Do you know what I've got to do? You can't return to City Island without a crew. If anything happened, I would be held responsible. So that means I must find at least eight bodies to make the trip back to City Island with you. Not only that, but lay on transportation to get them back here. The complement calls for ten. Can you two really handle this bucket?"

"We're here, sir, aren't we? No problem."

"Let's get this commissioning over with, then I'll see what I can round up."

The commissioning ceremony consisted of the lieutenant babbling something from a manual, then motioning Ted to raise the colors. This occupied five minutes. It took another fifteen for him to beg eight bodies from one of the destroyers under repair at a nearby berth.

Bravely flying the flag, *Tamarack*, now officially USS *Tamarack*, returned without misadventure to Nevins' Yard. Our arrival terminated a game of blackjack on the fantail that had started when we cast off. I never checked the logistics of the men's return to civilization.

It seemed odd that Len had not communicated with me or shown the slightest interest in his future floating home. I had plenty of more important things to worry about — like not pulling any blunders.

I phoned Commander Taintor to find out when the crew would arrive. He said their orders were being processed. They would be ordered to report to the ship at City Island within a week. I mentioned that *Tamarack* had functioned well with a two-man crew at the christening party, but if I didn't get some cleaning help pretty soon I was going to get way behind in my paper work. Now that I knew where the Supply Department was, I planned to order mess gear and bedding and find out how to obtain provisions. He chuckled and murmured something about pilgrim's progress.

The next morning, before I had time to telephone the Supply Department, they functioned unexpectedly, and in a big way. Ted reported that a five-ton Navy truck at the gate had a shipment for us. Where did we want it unloaded? We went ashore to see what goodies they had for *Tamarack*. The receipt that I was supposed to sign listed equipment for a crew of fifty men: fifty mattresses, mattress covers and pillows, mess gear for fifty, and galley gear enough for an ambitious restaurant. Ted and I opened cases and picked out what we thought the ship could use, plus one oak potato masher three feet long that must have weighed forty pounds. It seemed a useful weapon for an unarmed ship. This episode was definitely the Navy's slip. I only signed for what we kept. Maybe someday they will get their records straightened out.

Marine Basin in Brooklyn, near Coney Island, was an area the size of two city blocks enclosed on three sides by piers, with a single opening to Gravesend Bay. The shore end of the basin consisted of a fenced enclosure fronting on a street in which stood the large two-story building that housed the section administration offices and a parking lot.

I reported at 0900 to the section commander, a capable Regular Navy three-striper who had been called back to active duty from retirement for wartime service in the rank currently held by his classmates. This officer, I soon found out, ran a well-organized operation, liked by the skippers of Section Patrol craft attached. He was courteous, unhurried, well aware of the shortcomings and, within limits, tolerant of the reserve officers under his command.

After welcoming me to the section, he outlined the duties that *Tamarack* would be called on to perform. Two or three times a week a large number of merchant vessels, loaded for overseas, moved from the upper harbor down Ambrose Channel. When in the clear, they moved into assigned positions in a convoy formation under the watchful eye of the convoy commodore.

On convoy day *Tamarack* was to be on station at the seaward end of the channel at 0600 hours. On identifying the merchant ship carrying the commodore's flag *Tamarack* was to report to him for duty until released.

The next night at Marine Basin I left a call for 0400 hours as we had to be under way for convoy duty at 0500 hours. The liberty party was due back at 2400 hours. Ted had the watch from 0000 to 0400 hours. Promptly at 0400 hours he stuck his head in the door.

"Rise and shine, skipper. Eight bells. The chef needs you. He wants to set up breakfast."

"Breed and Wright?"

He nodded. "They came aboard two hours late, quiet but having drink taken."

"Tell the cook I'll be right along."

There were six berths in the quarters forward of the galley where the mess table was located, four lowers and two uppers. On the starboard side Len Breed had the transom berth forward with

George Wright in the pipe berth above him. When in use as an upper, its front was suspended by two lanyards from eyebolts overhead. It was hinged to the side of the ship, so that when lowered it formed a back for men sitting on the transom.

When I arrived, both men were asleep. The rest of the crew was sitting on the other transoms or standing in the galley silently awaiting my arrival in a high state of expectancy.

"Breed and Wright," I said quietly, "hit the deck. That's an order."

Wright turned over, presenting his back. Breed opened a bloodshot eye. "Oh, go to hell, captain." Neither made a start to leave his berth.

I picked up a carving knife, cut the forward line suspending the pipe berth, then stepped back out of the way and cut the other line, dumping the berth with Wright in it on top of Breed. Its edge drew blood from Breed's forehead. Wright's two hundred pounds bounced from Breed's belly to the floor. They struggled to their feet.

Breed, with clenched fists, looked murderous. I knew from college days that he had the reputation of having a dangerous temper. Wright just looked surprised and stupid.

I still kept my voice down. "You two are in the Navy, though you don't act like it. You are subject to my orders. You have just failed to acknowledge an order in the proper manner. You are both restricted to the ship for one week. If I don't find a change in your attitudes by that time, I shall have you both transferred to boot camp. Also, you will have to find out how to splice because you are to splice new lines on that pipe berth. Now here is another order. Straighten out this bedding and get dressed. Acknowledge."

Wright looked at Len, then at me, "Aye, aye," he said finally.

"Aye, aye what?"

"Aye, aye, sir."

"That's better. What's the matter, Breed, cat got your tongue?"

"Aye, aye, sir."

"Very well. Next time put more emphasis on the *sir*."

To the cook I said, "I'm going aft to shave. Send me a mug of coffee, will you? Two lumps."

"Aye, aye, Captain, *sir!*"

I remember this episode because it was the first time I had to exercise authority. This confrontation taught me that self-confidence is the essence of command.

Our convoy duty was to act as sheep dog in carrying messages to ships that had not reached their assigned positions, either because the ship had not identified her position in the formation or because she was awaiting a ship in her assigned column to take a forward position.

All the ships were deep-laden and slow in maneuvering. Guiding *Tamarack* often called for some nimble footwork to avoid collision. Signals, both by lamp and by semaphore, kept Ted on the jump. As the group moved slowly to the eastward, assigned escort vessels cast like hunting dogs, ahead and on the flank, searching for a lurking enemy submarine. When in final formation, the ships steamed in six or more parallel columns, usually five hundred yards apart, each ship keeping the same distance from the next ahead, six to eight ships in a column. The more valuable cargos, such as ammunition and fuel, were located toward the center of the formation, which proceeded to destination overseas at the speed of the slowest ship.

On convoy days *Tamarack* travelled many miles exhorting ships to take their positions, then reported back to the commodore. As changes in course of ships seeking their position were unpredictable, only unrelenting watchfulness on the part of *Tamarack*'s crew kept her out of trouble. This task was exacting enough in good weather, but in limited visibility the close escapes from collision were sometimes hair raising. The convoy was often forty miles at sea before *Tamarack* was released to return to port.

When not engaged in this duty, *Tamarack*, being unarmed, was used as a dispatch boat, carrying messengers or inspection parties back and forth between Brooklyn Navy Yard and other naval establishments in New York harbor, up the Hudson River, or at ports in Long Island Sound. Most of this work, the time being summer, was by daylight. Missions frequently had to be carried out in heavy fog, not the easiest job among the ferries and tows of New York harbor and the traffic of the East River. My careful compensation of the compass paid off; *Tamarack* acquired a reputation for accurate piloting.

Piloting and fixing position by celestial observation are two different ball games. I had no knowledge whatever of celestial navigation and was haunted by the fear that I might someday be ordered to an assignment requiring it.

Accordingly, three times that summer I sent in a request, through proper channels, to be transferred to a Navy school where navigation was taught. Each time the request was denied on the grounds that I could not be spared from present duty.

One pleasant summer evening while *Tamarack*, her day's chores completed, proceeded from the Navy Yard past the Brooklyn piers beneath Columbia Heights to our base at Marine Basin, I gazed up at the brownstone house overlooking New York harbor where I was born in 1891. The contrast between my present situation and the environment of that old residential street, a quiet backwater in the sprawling, teeming city always fascinated me. This night in my grandfather's house a few doors away the lights were on in the dining room. My train of thought led me to realize the incongruity of my lack of training and of the blind spots in my formal education for the responsibilities thrust on me by this Navy assignment. Rather bitterly I suddenly saw myself as I really was, a maverick.

Chapter 2
Background

THE HOUSES on Columbia Heights were built in the grand manner before the Civil War by men who had made fortunes in shipping. The Heights rise abruptly above warehouses that front on Furman Street across from piers that line the waterfront from the Navy Yard to Gowanus Canal. Small, formal gardens at the rear of the dwellings were built on the roofs of four-story warehouses. Windows facing west afforded a magnificent view of New York's busy harbor. When I was a child the distant Jersey shore was visible through a lofty tracery of spars and rigging of square-rigged sailing ships. Odors of tar, spices, and coffee mingled with the prevailing redolence of tidewater flowing darkly beneath the piers. Horse-drawn drays with steel tires rumbled over cobblestone paving.

I remember being lifted in the window at dusk to watch the Statue of Liberty lighted and to wonder at the height of the towers and the span of the new Brooklyn Bridge, which at that time dwarfed the skyline of lower Manhattan.

As late as World War I the heights was still a quiet, residential community, unchanged by time, its social lines as distinctly drawn as before ownership of the houses passed to the succeeding generation. These gentlemen, now elderly, inherited not only great wealth, but the ambition and ability to increase it in the fast-growing economy of the nation. They were the first generation to acquire leisure time and to become interested in literature and the arts.

Here lived Jays, Pierreponts, Lows, Stuyvesants, Hilliards,

Frothinghams, and Whites. My mother was a White, her mother a Hilliard, and her great-aunt a Frothingham. Mother was born to and accepted wealth and its responsibilities as a way of life. As long as she lived she was charming, generous, capricious, imperious, and spoiled. She married at eighteen.

My father, a strong, stocky, clear-eyed man of Scottish descent was still a bachelor at thirty-three. Born in an unfashionable part of Brooklyn into the loving family of a hard-working physician, he went to work at the age of thirteen in a paint factory and for the next six years regularly attended night school. Most of his earnings helped educate two younger brothers to become respectively a doctor and a lawyer. While still in his twenties my father was financially successful in both shipping and banking ventures. The year before his marriage he founded the banking firm of Moffat & White, backed by White capital.

It would be hard to imagine two people more utterly unlike in tastes and interests than my mother and father, but one thing they truly shared was devotion to their children.

Father's many interests took him to the West Coast and abroad. He was seldom home for long; we children looked forward eagerly to his visits, for he was a fascinating teller of bedtime stories. When he kissed us goodnight his close-trimmed, bristly moustache tickled, and he always smelled of the spotless starched shirts and cuffs that he affected.

The Moffat family were Swedenborgians. Father never drank or played cards. The only times he ever smoked was to blow warm cigarette smoke into an aching ear when one of us had an earache. The White family were Unitarians. The women attended church sporadically; their menfolk supported the cause only financially.

I remember asking Mother why we never went to church like other children.

"To go to church you have to have faith that the world is controlled by God. This is a very comforting belief, if you can find it for yourself. It is much too precious to be imposed on children by their elders. When you grow up I hope you will find a faith that will comfort you and convince you of a hereafter. I wish from the bottom of my heart I could find a faith. I never have been able to rationalize religious teachings. Some day you may find a faith in love, but not by going through the routine formulas of a church."

The first time I went to the communion rail with Sally I knew

Mother had missed one of the most uplifting experiences a human being can share.

As a young child I must have been an insufferable, self-conscious sissy. Mother made me memorize sentimental little poems to recite in front of the ladies who attended her formal afternoon teas. Produced by a uniformed nursemaid for these occasions, I was dressed in a Little Lord Fauntleroy costume, embroidered green tunic, short trousers, long black stockings, and patent leather pumps. My golden curls hung almost to my shoulders. The ladies always clapped politely and told Mother how angelic I looked. I daresay I simpered.

One day Father unexpectedly appeared at one of these tea parties. When my performance was finished he marched me straight to a nearby barber. He delivered me back to the party looking more like a boy. Mother burst into tears. "George, how could you!" she wailed. At that moment I felt a new bond with my father. He hugged me briefly, bowed to the ladies, and without a word went upstairs.

When I was nine we moved from the hallowed precincts of Columbia Heights to New York City. After a year at Miss Borden's School for small children, I attended private day schools for boys where I was miserably unhappy. Due to a glandular deficiency I had been growing too fast. At the age of eleven, weighing a scant ninety pounds, I was the tallest boy in school, a freak and a weakling, preyed upon by older, sadistic bullies. The masters, if indeed they noticed, did not appear to care.

I lived in such fear of being repeatedly and surreptitiously hurt that I did not properly concentrate on lessons. Consequently I flunked out. I had been badly spoiled at home; now I was a crybaby and a coward, a bitter, introspective loner with no friends.

Summer vacations were a respite. We did not always go to the Adirondacks. One memorable summer when I was ten, at Quogue, Long Island, on the sheltered waters of Shinnecock Bay, unbeknownst to Mother I hired a sailing skiff and taught myself to sail, with little brother Donald as reluctant crew. It was a proud day when I invited Father to come with us. He was surprised at my progress. Brushing aside Mother's objections, he chartered a small catboat, which I sailed happily the rest of the summer. From then on, boats were a dominating influence in my life.

Lake George, New York, became the family's permanent

summer home. Here there was no sailing. Instead, I became intrigued with marine engines and motorboat racing. For the first time I found friends of my age with whom to share interests.

The winter that followed I was placed in a different school. I was now six feet fall, still not gaining much weight and still considered by the other boys to be a freak. There was less persecution, but I remained a loner, doing badly in my studies.

This was my last year in a city school. The following September I entered Middlesex, a boarding school in Concord, Massachusetts, there to spend three years preparing for Harvard, the alma mater of the Whites.

The summer of 1907 I was not to spend at Lake George, to which I had eagerly looked forward, but at Professor Allen's tutoring school at Seal Harbor on Mount Desert Island, Maine, thus to be better prepared scholastically for Middlesex. My family departed for Europe and I was shipped off to Maine. I felt like an outcast, alone, frightened of the unknown and unsure of myself.

As things turned out it proved to be a happy and fruitful summer. The professor, a member of the faculty of Columbia University, was relaxed and sympathetic. The Allens took a few boys into their summer home for tutoring. This couple were gifted teachers who understood boys. Only seven others were enrolled, all tutoring for college entrance exams. As they were older, their interest outside school hours was mainly girls. They were aloof but friendly. In that household I felt welcome and unafraid. Mrs. Allen, a motherly little woman, seemed to take pleasure in filling our stomachs.

Professor Allen soon discovered my obsession with boats. To my surprise he suggested that I find some sort of craft in which to spend my free hours. Thus began a wonderful adventure, which with his help, laid substantial groundwork for future Navy experience.

I found, moored in the harbor, a twelve-foot, decked launch which appeared to be complete except for an engine. This was being used as its mooring. The owner, a laconic native, said it saved him buying an anchor; the engine was beyond repair and was not even much of a mooring. After consulting the professor I offered a deal: for the use of the boat for the summer I would buy from Sears Roebuck, for $35.50, and install, a new two-horsepower engine identical with the old one, to become the boatowner's property at the end of the season.

Two weeks later the new engine was installed, and I was the captain of my own ship. In the meantime, under the professor's direction I had acquired a local chart, a pair of parallel rules, and a second-hand dory compass. He showed me how to read the chart and the compass and to lay courses. His conditions for my using the boat were that I should be back in school in time for breakfast, and after school hours in time for supper.

Every day at first crack of dawn, regardless of weather, I climbed silently out of my ground floor window to go seafaring. When it was foggy, as it often was, I did not venture beyond the sound of the bell buoy at the entrance of the harbor. This first taste of responsibility was heady stuff. By trial and error I learned the rudiments of piloting; more important I saw the practical application of learning, which had never before occurred to me. I began, too, to make progress with my school work. There were no classes; this was teaching at its best.

At Middlesex, where organized exercise was compulsory, I avoided contact sports like football and hockey for fear of being hurt. I went out for rowing, which involved six months on rowing machines before getting on the water. After three school years of rowing, the last two on the crew, my growth eased off at six feet two inches. I was a well-coordinated one hundred seventy-five pounds of lean muscle.

Still a loner, but no longer picked on, at last I felt physically adequate.

In 1909 when I entered Harvard the elective system was at its peak. Of the sixteen full courses required for graduation only four basics were compulsory: English, government, economics, and history. The other twelve could be selected by the undergraduate who either chose subjects that happened to interest him or that were rumored to be "cinches." No courses in mathematics were required for a degree. Math had always been my worst subject, probably because I had never been taught its purpose. So, in school I never got beyond plane geometry, and that with a barely passing mark. Accordingly, I avoided like the plague electing any math courses. Those courses I did elect, because for one reason or another they intrigued my curiosity, included such unrelated subjects as meteorology, physiology, mechanical drawing, diesel engineering, fine arts, and as many courses in English composition as I could qualify for. In my subsequent career in the Navy the most valuable education I received at Harvard proved to be in meteorology, diesel engineering, and the ability to express myself in writing.

Generally speaking, I regarded the college curriculum as the price to be paid for time spent in far more intriguing activities, such as being a scoutmaster and fixing cars. The resulting poor marks more than once put me temporarily on probation.

The summer after my sophomore year was the turning point in my life when I fell in love with the girl I was to be married to for sixty-one years.

I had been invited to join a leisurely cruise in a twenty-eight-foot yawl without power, the *Brant*, owned by two undergraduate brothers named Ross. Thorvald, the older, was a competent skipper and all-round seaman in spite of the handicap of two withered legs. On board he could dispense with his wheel chair; he moved on hands and knees. On the rare occasions when he went ashore he was carried on his brother Harold's back. They were powerful men. Harold, my classmate, was my height and Thorvald, had he been able to stand, would probably have been even taller. They were half-Danish, which probably accounted for their instinctive love of the sea.

Thorvald, a brilliant scholar, was an enthusiastic and gifted instructor. He was a class ahead of us and had already made Phi Beta Kappa. From no other source could I have learned in the space of two months as much about seamanship, ship handling, weather, and tide forecasting, and how to live comfortably and eat well with limited facilities. The Rosses were great men. One day at anchor at North Haven, Maine, Harold recalled having met at a dance in Boston an attractive girl named Sally DeCamp, daughter of the famous painter Joseph DeCamp who had a summer place nearby. By chance the DeCamp family launch passed close enough for Harold to recognize the girl and hail. The *Brant* was invited to follow to Crockett's Cove where we would be welcome to anchor. At the time I was below shaving and did not get a good look at the girl in the red blazer who was aboard with her father and some younger children. Anyway, I was not particularly interested in girls.

The day was sunny with a light head wind. When we anchored in the cove an hour later the family had long since gone up to the

Sally and Sandy Moffat, May 1913

Moffat at ease on the bridge of *SC No. 143*, 1918

Chapter 3

Subchaser No. 77,
New York—New London

LATE IN DECEMBER I received a message telling me to phone the personnel officer. Commander Taintor said that orders were being processed detaching me from *Tamarack* to command a new 110-foot subchaser scheduled for duty overseas.

I was aghast. "But, sir, I don't know how to navigate. Every request I have made through channels to be sent to a navigation school has been denied on the grounds that I could not be spared from present duty. On any deep water assignment I'd have to know how to navigate."

"Don't worry. Every one of the chasers will be fitted out and trained at New London, Connecticut, before going overseas. That training includes a comprehensive course in celestial navigation."

A ton of worry was lifted off my soul.

"Who relieves me on *Tamarack*, sir? I think DeCamp is capable. To be sure, he is a petty officer, but he knows the ship and the duty inside and out. Couldn't you swear him in as an ensign as you did me?"

The commander laughed. "So I could. The thought had occurred to me, too. *Tamarack* has turned in a good record. I am glad to have your opinion of DeCamp. By the way, Breed and Wright have requested transfers. That should make DeCamp's job easier, wouldn't you say?"

A week later, a division of six subchasers, fresh from the yard of a builder up the Hudson River, arrived at Marine Basin. The

34

local tug had to break ice to work them into their berths. The thermometer stood at zero.

On January 4 orders arrived assigning me to command *SC No. 77*, one of the newly arrived group. I went over with my orders to inform the ensign commanding that I was there to relieve him.

The 110-foot subchasers were developed by the Navy Department to cope with the growing menace of enemy submarines, as well as to replace smaller craft worn out in the service of the French navy. Designed by Commander A. Loring Swasey, USNR, in civilian life a talented naval architect, before war's end four hundred fifty of them were produced by fifty building yards in the eastern United States. Vital statistics of these little ships are set forth in the Appendix.

It speaks well for the basic design that although many were lost by fire, collision, or enemy action, not one was lost through stress of weather.

The skipper of *No. 77* looked at me stupidly, "I think there is some mistake," he said, "I am in command of this chaser and I know nothing of being relieved."

"You do now," I said, handing him my orders. "Please muster your crew at once, so that I may read these orders to them as required by regulations."

This he made no move to do, so I went to the forehatch and called down, "The captain wants all hands on deck. Move!"

The crew, a sullen, undernourished-looking lot, straggled out and fell into some semblance of a line. Thereupon I read my orders. Their faces were a study. I had a feeling they were thoroughly discouraged. I soon found that they would have considered any change one for the better.

After reading the orders I told them that they would get a square deal and that in return I expected the same treatment, that *No. 77* would be just what they made it, and that it was my intention to make her the best kept and most efficient chaser in the force; if they were disposed to have it so, it would be brought about.

I told the chief boatswain's mate and the chief machinist's mate to follow me below to the officers' quarters and dismissed the rest. As the late skipper headed for the office I asked him to have his belongings cleared so that I could move aboard by 1600 hours.

Then I had an informal talk with my two leading petty officers, primarily to find out the condition of the men and material in their

keep within a length of the next ahead. The night was dark and bitterly cold. Solid pans of ice setting out of Gardiners Bay and The Race forced the column to find devious channels where the ice was broken.

An ebbing tide carries all the water in Long Island Sound through The Race at four knots. Against this current we were making slow progress. Cross bearings on several lights indicated that we had only a mile or so to go to be out of the strength of the current. At this point Ayers stopped the column and passed the word for all chasers to anchor for the night. This decision was the more stupid because The Race is the deepest area in the sound. No anchors could hold us against the combination of current and countless tons of ice it discharged into Block Island Sound.

I ordered both anchors unshackled and a few fathoms of the empty chains hung over the bow. The guess was a good one, for Ayers turned his searchlight on each chaser to see that they had complied with his orders. From the rapidity with which bearings on the lights changed, it was obvious that *No.* 77 was being carried out into Block Island Sound at the same speed as the chasers with their anchors down. We found out later that the other chasers lost their anchors and most of their chains.

As we were being set clear of any hazards to navigation, there was nothing further to do. I set a watch and spent the remainder of the night with as many of the crew as could jam into the quarters aft trying to get warm from the galley stove. By keeping the hatches shut we managed to raise the temperature in this part of the ship to 15° F.

Morning dawned clear with a brisk northwest wind and a further drop in temperature to 15° below zero. We were almost in the middle of Block Island Sound, frozen in solid. Fisher's Island was a lavender streak on the horizon to the north; Block Island barely discernible to the east.

While some of the crew amused themselves by building a fire on the ice a hundred feet from the ship for their camera records, I walked half a mile to Ayers' chaser to report all well with *No.* 77.

By 1200 hours a patch of open water in the northwest gradually enlarged toward us until three hours later we were free. Ayers seemed to have lost his bearings entirely, for he headed for Point Judith instead of New London. Fifteen minutes later he dropped back to hail me by megaphone.

Block Island Sound, frozen over, December 1917

from the galley to the mess table, which was set with a white cloth. Having always been in my own ship I had had little opportunity to observe the household organization of other vessels. During a very pleasant meal I made copious mental notes for the improvement of *No.* 77.

Chapter 4
Subchaser No. 143, *New York — Overseas*

THE SECOND morning after our arrival I was summoned to the office. Commander Spafford waved a dispatch at me.

"Close the door, Moffat, and sit down."

Although sensing something important I was not prepared for his next words.

"You have been accorded an unusual opportunity. You are hereby detached from command of SC *No. 77* and will at once assume command of SC *No. 143*, sailing on foreign service at 0600 hours tomorrow. The commanding officer of *No. 143* unfortunately lost his leg in an accident yesterday. He will therefore not be present for you to relieve him. Muster the crew yourself and read your orders to them."

My stunned reaction was mixed, disappointment at being detached from a half-finished job just when *No. 77* was beginning to shape up, and alarm that I would now not be able to attend the navigation course. Then came the surging realization that I would have to say goodbye to Sally.

"Aye, aye, sir," I said stiffly, "I must tell you that I have not yet had the opportunity to learn navigation and therefore I am not qualified."

He answered, drily, "You'll know how by the time you reach the other side. Dismissed."

Suddenly I recalled that *No. 143* was in George's division. This was a reassuring thought; I knew I could rely on his experience and advice. I stopped at the telephone booth to tell Sally, with a lump

charge of the stowing. Carney requested permission to spend the evening ashore. I caught a barely perceptible nod from Dancy and acquiesced. As a matter of curiosity I asked him why he wanted to go ashore when there was so much to be done. He said he had arranged to be married at eight o'clock.

In private life he ran a merry-go-round at Coney Island. How he had succeeded in getting a commission in the Naval Reserve is beyond me, and in the crowded hours that we had together I never found time to ask him.

At nine o'clock as I started uptown to meet Sally, I was handed a letter from *SC No. 77*, which I still treasure. It read as follows:

U.S.S.C. No. 77
Feb. 20, 1918

From crew of *SC No. 77*
To: Our beloved Captain and Friend, Mr. Moffat

We write these few lines to express our sorrow on having to part with a man who has treated us as an officer, a friend, and a man. Words cannot express too clearly our own regret on having to part after we all were so happy and contented. We make one wish and pray that we get another man like yourself, and as long as you live you can remember your old faithful crew of the *SC No. 77* will always remember you and your kindness towards us.

A word before we part. We the crew you know wish you the greatest success in any undertaking you may take and wish you all the good luck in the world, and hope we may sometime again in the future be shipmates once more.

Your grateful crew
[Signed by twenty men]

George's wife had already arrived. At the Mohican where we had engaged rooms we found Sally, who in spite of the weather had driven from Flushing in our Model T Ford instead of taking the train.

That night in the privacy of our room there were so many plans to be discussed and decisions to be made against a separation of unforeseeable length that it was past midnight before we could relax in the warmth of each other's arms. No words were necessary.

46

At four o'clock we were up and dressed to walk together through dark streets to the pier where Bertha and George waited. A bitter wind drove fine snow horizontally. As civilians were not admitted through the gate, our final farewells were unsatisfactorily made under a street lamp. For eleven months I carried the memory of my Sally smiling and waving and trying to comfort Bertha who was dissolved in tears. It was bitterly cold, with the makings of a northeast blizzard starting. I think George was as glad as I that the approach to the pier was badly lighted. We were due to pull out in two hours.

At the first crack of daylight the departing chasers took positions off the end of the pier to follow a tug that was to break ice for us out of the harbor. All the ranking officers in the district were on the pierhead to see the departure for the war zone of the first detachment of this new arm of the service. There was not much time to feel any inspiration in the moment. I was grateful for the distracting activity of last minute details.

The tug pulled out, followed one by one by the chasers soon swallowed up in the swirling snow. *No. 143* was last in column. A second tug along the side of the dock thrust a cake of ice at our stern just as our rudder was put hard over to swing clear. A sharp crack, and the quartermaster spun the wheel without avail. The steering gear had carried away. We backed up to the dock and put out our lines. In an instant the base engineer officer was aboard to ascertain the trouble, while the senior officers fired useless questions from the dock.

We found that the teeth in the rack and pinion of the steering gear had sheered off clean, necessitating a new rack. Although the boats were supposed to be of standard construction, with all parts interchangeable, it so happened that *No. 143* was equipped with an odd type of gear that could not be replaced with the stock gear without considerable alteration. My invaluable Dancy at this juncture said that *No. 142*, which had been sold to the French government, was built by the same yard, and that undoubtedly had the same make of gear. *No. 142* was lying on the other side of the State Pier with a skeleton French crew aboard. The engineer officer, Dancy, and I dashed aboard and found an identical apparatus installed. The French crew, who didn't understand a word of English, were mystified at our excitement, but when they saw us start to demolish the officers' quarters with a hammer and crowbar

fixtures on the deck. The depth charges in the racks were moved below to the magazine.

At dark the wind piped up, presently blowing half a gale with a merciless rising note in the rigging. By daylight *No. 143* was making heavy weather. Dancy reported that we were leaking from the pounding, but that the pumps were keeping ahead of it.

At dawn of the third day out, at last in the warmth of the Gulf Stream, the eastern horizon, banked with dark clouds above a low lying streak of red, indicated a sunrise stillborn. Flying scud overhead and rain and spray driving horizontally bore evidence of a new gale that whistled out of the northeast.

Just before dark a vicious sea struck the pilot house so solidly that it groaned, smashing windows on the port side and forward. The two men on duty were saved from injury from flying glass by their thick, heavy-weather gear and hoods. The man at the wheel yelled, "Steering gear is stuck. Can't move it!"

For the past two hours the wheel had been held hard over in an endeavor to bring the ship's bow more nearly into the sea. Now it appeared that the vertical shaft between the steering gear and the rack and pinion below had bent enough to lock the gear in its hard-over position, caused by the whole structure of the house having acquired a cant to starboard. Fortunately, the hatch in the deck that gave access to the officers' quarters below had a high coaming, which prevented the inches of water and broken glass sloshing over the floor from getting below. The hatch was closed.

Due to foresight of the designer, the rudder stock on which the steering quadrant was mounted was above the deck, as were the steering cables leading forward on each side to the pilot house. The rudder stock above the quadrant was fitted to take an emergency tiller. This six-foot, hundred-pound iron contraption we managed to mount while the deck was swept knee deep by seas. The boatboom tackles were taken from the mast and lashed to the tiller on one end and to a rail stanchion on the other. The hauling part of each was led forward to the lee of the bridge for swinging the tiller by hand. Then, with difficulty, the cable to the locked steering gear was cut with a hack saw. We still could not head up, but at least we had control of the rudder.

By dark we had cut away the weather cloths on the bridge and nailed the heavy canvas over the broken pilot house windows.

During the night, intercepted radio messages had brought

dismaying information of nine subchasers disabled and drifting, and of the tug *Cherokee* fifty miles astern, which sent an SOS saying that she would be unable to stay afloat until morning. Then a sea that smashed the hatch of our radio room put our set out of commission. Our own *No. 143* and the tug *Mariner* were the only two surviving ships under way half a mile apart on a wild and lonesome ocean striving desperately to hold their bows to the seas.

Fear for my ship and for my own life lay like a quivering lump in my belly. Never had I seen anything like these racing seas, backs streaked with foam, tumbling crests that folded like breakers on a beach. From time to time a fiercer squall transplanted a whole crest bodily to the back of the sea to leeward. *No. 143* staggered up the face of each wave to be cuffed viciously and buried in a smother of white water that cast the hull broadside into the trough, there to fetch it up with a shattering jolt. I did not see how any structure built of wood could survive the wrenching onslaught of these great marching seas that lifted, battered, and dropped their victim in an endless succession of dizzying falls while the decks shouldered off tons of churning water. Half-blinded by driven spray, I could hear even above the storm the creaking and groaning of the tortured hull.

No. 143 had suffered considerable damage. A manhole cover aft had been carried away, flooding the lazarette to the deck. This meant that all food stores but canned stuff and hams were ruined. Decks were swept clean of ventilators. The openings had been stuffed with signal flags. The only collision mat had been nailed over the forward end of the radio room. The wherry, or twelve-foot lifeboat, still in its chocks amidships, was split from end to end, disintegrating piecemeal. Lifelines were rigged from the wheelhouse all the way aft. The crew, except for helmsman and engineers, were lashed along the lee side of the house, most of them in a torpor of misery, drenched and weary, too seasick to feel hunger or thirst, too numbed to know fear.

I saw that the *Mariner* was down by the bow, taking terrific punishment. Her radio shack on the boat deck was crumpled like an old cardboard box, her lifeboat was gone, and her funnel swayed crazily. As the seas broke against her, I could see under her stern, lifted high before each plunge, the big propeller still slowly turning. All at once I realized with horror that the *Mariner* was foundering and that we were unable to change course to help. *No.*

With a feeling akin to panic I took stock of the situation. Darkness was two hours away, our radio was out, our present position was unknown, and we had no ship to follow. Too, I began to doubt whether structurally we could survive another night. Appalled by the loneliness of this wild welter of water, I felt suddenly lethargic with fear and fatigue.

Mr. Carney chose this moment to go completely to pieces. He clasped me around the legs weeping, screaming, begging to be saved from drowning. The men within earshot watched wide-eyed and uneasy.

I was shocked to the core. The psychological reaction to fear is anger. I found myself abruptly overwhelmed by a consuming rage that instantly purged me of my own fears. That anger filled me with a sudden resurgence of strength and determination, aware that Carney's panic called for instant action. I beckoned to Chadwick and a flat-faced, husky Polish youth. Then in a ringing voice of authority I hardly recognized, I gave the necessary order. It was in language unbecoming an officer and a gentleman.

"This bastard is detached from duty, under arrest. Get him below. If he won't go down the hatch, pitch him down head first!"

Chadwick grinned. "Aye, aye, sir!" he said heartily. "Come on, Ski, you heard the man!"

As the long night wore through its weary hours the wind perceptibly diminished and the seas, no longer breaking, gradually lengthened. I was bone tired; I couldn't remember when I had last slept. I tried to focus my mind on how to reach Bermuda. By the lengthening seas I assumed that *No. 143* had now left the Gulf Stream, again on the compass course steered before the storm. This was close to the course on which the *Wadena* had disappeared.

At last one encouraging idea occurred to me. I recalled the spectacular leeway of the ships during the rescue as evidenced by the illusion of the life ring moving against the wind; therefore, I concluded, the strength of the stream setting directly against the northeaster had quite possibly offset the subchaser's leeway. Keeping the bow headed into the seas had in fact caused her to move crabwise across the stream, thus remaining approximately on the original line.

At 0200 hours I tried to plot our assumed position on the chart. I measured off the distance to Bermuda and calculated that if I was destined to find the island at all, by running two engines I could make a landfall before dark, steering the present course.

Engine-room bells clanged; the tired midship engine was given a rest and the two wing engines, to the sound of thuttering exhausts, imparted new life to the ship as *No. 143* picked up speed.

I was observing the dawn of a beautiful new day when Mr. Carney burst into the wheel house, pushing aside two men who sought to restrain him. Carney glared at them. He had made no effort to clean himself. He addressed me in a voice that was arrogant and unabashed.

"Good morning, Moffat," he said briskly, "I'll take over the watch now. You must be very tired."

I drew a long breath, the eyes of the men on me.

"Captain Moffat to you," I answered crisply. "Mr. Carney, as I told you yesterday, you are under arrest. That means that you are relieved of all duties. If you leave your quarters again, you will be handcuffed there. You are a dirty, stinking mess. Now get the hell out of my sight!" Carney bolted below like a rabbit. The men exchanged pleased glances.

Morale rose with the sun. I ordered all hands to shave and change. Dancy brought word that, except for the lazarette which was being bailed by bucket brigade, all bilges would be clear within the hour. Hatches were opened to balmy sunshine, wet gear was spread to dry and the ship trailed her white wake across an undulating ocean of peaceful blue. The crew's conversation again reverted to women.

By 1200 hours canned goods dredged from the lazarette enabled the cook to produce a hot meal of corned beef, spaghetti Italian style, and coffee sweetened with condensed milk. To me, canned peaches were the finest dessert that had ever passed my lips. Sparks reported the likelihood that the radio could be restored to operation.

Time passed in normal shipboard duties. A magnificent sunset colored the western horizon while dusk crept up the eastern sky. Dancy appeared on the bridge to inquire casually what time I expected to make a landfall. He reported that at present speed fuel remained for four hours steaming.

I replied as casually, hoping that my voice implied a confidence I didn't feel, "Anytime, now, Dancy. Lookout, let me know the minute you sight Gibb's Hill Light." It sounded better to be specific. Nothing was visible on the vast and lonely seascape.

the trans-Atlantic passage from Bermuda to Gibraltar via Ponta Delgada in the Azores.

The commanding officer, also in command of all chasers attached, was Captain Nelson, USN, known throughout the Navy as "Juggy" Nelson, a hell-for-leather destroyer skipper with a well-deserved record as a leader. Whether his nickname derived from his shape or from a discriminating taste in liquor I do not know. It could have been either.

Leonidas flew the flag of SOPA, meaning "senior officer present afloat." She lay at anchor off the dockyard, an old Navy gunboat of about six thousand tons, of Spanish War vintage.

A letter from Captain Nelson was promptly distributed to each subchaser skipper, a pleasantly informal letter that expressed the hope that each of us would find time to pay him a visit. *Leonidas* was to be our floating base until we arrived at our eventual destination. The paymaster would carry our accounts and the supply officer would issue stores and parts as needed. Enough spare parts for our machinery were carried to equip the permanant base to be established ashore at an unspecified eventual destination. Postmaster, New York, would forward all mail for the chasers to *Leonidas* for distribution. He said not to hesitate to call for any technical assistance needed. Life began to look considerably rosier.

I was in urgent need for a replacement for Carney, and wanted to make a couple of other changes in personnel, so I decided to pay a visit to the captain. George Atwood accompanied me. This was not a regulations procedure. We should have referred any requests through our squadron commander, in whom none of us had confidence.

We were ushered into Captain Nelson's presence without delay. His desk was in "the great Cabin" with stern windows. He came forward to meet us with a broad smile and outstretched hand. I have seldom met a man so able instantly to impart confidence. After introductions he told us to pull up chairs and have a smoke.

"You've had a rough trip, boys. I want to know what I can do for your ships."

We did not tell any tales out of school, but his skilfull questioning gave him a pretty good idea of how much the group needed leadership.

He interrupted when I told him about Carney, still restricted to the ship under technical arrest.

"When you go back, pack him up and have him escorted aboard here to report to the master at arms. I shall send him home by first available transportation to be released from the service as emotionally unfit. No charges, no fuss. My medical officer will attend to the necessary forms." It was as easy as that.

"And by the way," he added, "I have just the replacement for him, a warrant boatswain USNR who was executive officer aboard the *Mariner*. His skipper has high praise for him. I talked with him myself and was favorably impressed. I'll have a set of orders cut and get him over to you this afternoon. His name is Peter Connolly.

"You will also have a new squadron commander; Lieutenant N. A. Johnson, USN, commanding *Subchaser No. 226*. He is a mustang who served with me when he was a chief warrant officer, so I know him well. He now holds a well-deserved temporary commission as senior lieutenant. I have confidence that he will do a competent job."

Before George and I took our leave I had traded two impossibly chronic seasickers for the promise of a second signalman and a mess attendant, neither of which *No. 143* rated.

Connolly reported for duty wearing a ready-made civilian blue serge suit and his officer's cap. He hastened to explain that he was having a uniform made in Hamilton. He had been in working clothes when taken off the *Mariner* and had lost all his possessions except what he stood in. His orders and his pilot's license he had put in his cap.

From our first meeting I knew that he and I were going to get along together. He proved to be always the same: watchful, respectful, and forever on the job, usually with a good sized quid of tobacco in his cheek. He was a tall, lean man of my age, with blue eyes and an aggressive chin, in civilian life a licensed Hudson River tug boat pilot. The crew liked and respected him because he was as honest with them as he was with himself, and because he had sense enough to remain aloof.

The dockyard straightened the pilot house and secured it with steel cables and turnbuckles against a similar accident. The twelve-foot lifeboat was beyond repair. It was replaced by a used one, British built, of about the same dimensions but more sturdy construction.

Glass was replaced in the pilot-house windows. On the recommendation of a British officer who had served in small craft,

understand what was wanted. His job was to look after Connolly and me, keep our quarters and our clothes clean, serve our food, and generally help the cook. He was equipped with a guitar, which considerably augmented the ship's orchestra of mandolin, mouth organ, and clarinet. The crew called him Florence. He gave me to understand he had not set foot on shore for a month. His joy at being given liberty his first day aboard was pathetic.

At long last in all respects ready for sea, *Leonidas* departed Bermuda with her brood of twenty-four subchasers, making four squadrons. As we took off from St. David's Head we passed the inbound steamer *Charibdis* from New York, and with a pang realized that it carried precious mail that might not reach us for weeks or even months.

George Atwood and I each now commanded a division of three chasers in the same squadron. We had a fuel radius of about one thousand miles in average weather. The distance to our next port, Ponta Delgada, was 1,600 nautical miles. Orders directed us to rendezvous with a tanker half-way to the Azores from which we would refuel and top off with water.

We rolled monotonously over a windswept, summer sea, organized into watches of four hours on and four hours off. Small personal frictions magnified out of all proportion. One day my listening post informed me there was a fight brewing between the engine-room gang and the deck crew. The black gang used the wrong length of hose to pump engine-room bilges and when the deck gang started to hose decks with their rightful hose their spotless decks were spotted with oil. Human beings are highly strung things, particularly men without women.

What might have been a fist fight was promptly quelled by Connolly. It seemed to me they were acting like a bunch of intestinally upset children. That set me to wondering what Sally would do with upset children. The answer came to me in a flash. I had all hands mustered on deck except one man in the engine room and a man at the wheel. I sent Florin for the largest cooking spoon he could find and faced the crew with a gallon bottle under my arm. Without explanation I downed a spoonful and beckoned to our big Polish boy called Ski, administered his dose, and had him stand beside me. I felt sure that when I got the castor oil into three or four of them, they would see to it that recalcitrants, if any, would get theirs. Unfortunately, I forgot that there was but one head for twenty-four men who had been dosed at approximately the same time. The accidents that ensued were greeted with roars of laughter.

By the next morning headaches had vanished, smiles appeared, and some of the younger men were playing tag around the deck, whooping like the kids they were.

Two of the men, however, were in a bad way. After three two-ounce doses of castor oil brought no results, I semaphored the flagship, "Unofficial from Moffat *No. 143* to Doctor Calloway. What to do when three doses castor oil don't work. End." I expected him to reply "Caesarian section," because that was about his line of humor. The answer came, "Three heaping tablespoons epsom salts dissolved in one glass hot water. Will stand by for results."

Results came in about thirty minutes. Florin was one of the victims. He was pathetically bewildered, feeling sick. Not being able to speak much English he acted like a little sick animal.

The next morning when I came on deck before dawn, a black night it was, too, Florin was on deck aft dumping buckets of salt water over himself, singing and having a perfectly lovely time. Then he played his guitar until 0600 hours. From his flashing smile I judged his recovery was complete.

Two days of rough weather again produced seasickers, including myself. Bouillion cubes and crackers, usually on the third try, was all the nourishment I could keep down.

The next day the wind dropped and the sea smoothed out. It was the day we were scheduled to meet the tanker. There she was, a great sow waiting for the hungry piglets. Unbelievably the sea was like a lake while, three at a time on each side the chasers took on two thousand gallons of gasoline each and filled their water tanks. The tanker's cooks must have been up all night, for each chaser was presented with a dozen loaves of fresh bread. They disappeared in one meal — delicious!

The sixteenth day out from Bermuda we sighted far to port the ten thousand foot peak of Pico, the northernmost island of the Azores. Our estimated distance to Ponta Delgada was one hundred fifty miles. The following morning as we approached land we ran into a wall of fog reminiscent of that along the coast of Maine.

The cook served us a special breakfast to celebrate our landfall. His name was George Washington Loden, and he will remain in my memory as one of the unsung heroes of the war. He was a poor

63

white sharecropper from Texas who walked fifty miles to a Navy recruiting office to enlist. Asked what branch he wanted to get into, he looked bewildered. The recruiter said, "Fine, you are a seaman, striking for ship's cook," and shipped him off to boot camp.

When he reported for duty aboard *No. 143* as acting cook George had never prepared a meal in his life. Webb, the gunner's mate, who could turn a hand to almost anything, took over the feeding of the crew until by the time *No. 143* reached New London, he had taught George to cook. This gentle, awkward youth, stuck to his job even when seasick, preparing a hot meal for twenty-six men, sometimes coming on deck a dozen times to retch.

As likely as not when everything was finally ready, the deck two inches deep in slopped food, broken china, and sloshing salt water, the ship would give an extra lurch and over would go the big cauldron containing the whole meal. Without a complaint except a sigh, he would turn to, clean up the mess, and start the meal all over again. Most men would sit down and cry. A knock would come on the pilot-house door and George's pale, set face would appear, "Mr. Moffat, sir, chow will be kind of late. There is a right smart motion and my pot done tipped over on me." That is all, while I was having trouble staying lashed in my little seat.

George told me that the girl he was engaged to sent back his ring because "men ought not to fight." She had married another man who was promptly drafted. Censoring his letters, I knew that it took George two years to save up for that ring. I didn't see her letter to him, but it must have been a stinker. When he brought me the ring he said simply, "Mr. Moffat I done lost my girl. Will you keep this for me? Tain't no use to me now." His eyes were full of tears.

I said, "Listen, George, that girl would never have made you happy. It will be a lonesome feeling for a while, but you will find you are well out of it."

"Yes, sir, I reckon you're right, but I sure did set a heap store by that little girl."

He wrote his mother that he hoped he would get killed in the war, that he thought every man in the country ought to enlist. He told me that other than his mother and his girl, I was the only human being who had ever tried to help him. He said, "I never forget these things," and went back to his little inferno aft.

Ponta Delgada is the seaport of São Miguel, the largest island in the Azores group. The harbor is long and narrow, created by a wide breakwater parallel to the west shore from which lighters transfer cargo to or from ships moored fore and aft between great mooring buoys. There is room for a merchant ship to be turned by tugs to be headed toward the entrance before securing to the buoys. There are no offshore hazards in approaching the end of the breakwater, but entering requires an abrupt 90° left turn. Cargo is stacked the length of the breakwater along a trucking road that ends at a lighthouse. The town lies along the other side of the harbor on a gently sloping hillside extending to cultivated fields.

As we approached, our squadron was sent ahead in line abreast within visual distance of each other. Visibility in the fog was no more than fifty yards. We could smell the land, the fragrant odor of vegetation. The sea was flat calm. Presently on signal the six chasers stopped simultaneously to listen. Curiously enough, there was no sound signal on the lighthouse.

Suddenly the silence was shattered by an abrupt but unmistakable noise up ahead, a Model T Ford being started. We approached gingerly. In a few moments the lighthouse was revealed, the Ford Model T driving off along the breakwater.

Leonidas moored between two buoys. The chasers moored by divisions, each division swinging three abreast to a single buoy.

As soon as we were moored a ship's lifeboat sculled by a single oar came alongside. One of the two Portuguese natives aboard spoke English. He explained that they would collect all our dirty clothes for the laundry ashore and return them washed the next morning. Most of the clothes were stenciled with the men's names. I told them to keep a careful list of what each sent.

The next morning is memorable because of two momentous events: The laundry burned down during the night and we received orders detaching *No. 143* and five other chasers from *Leonidas* for a new assignment. This group under the command of Lieutenant Johnson included *No. 177.* It seemed George Atwood and I were not to be separated, for which, because of my navigational limitations, I gave fervent thanks.

When the laundry boat returned it was full of charred clothing, some in bits and pieces, from which the crew was asked to pick what they could identify. There proved to be no redress.

When the skippers of six chasers were summoned to the *Leonidas* we suspected that there must be something afoot, but the information that we were to be detached was a thunderbolt. Captain Nelson waved a despatch at us when we reported to him in the great cabin. He came right to the point.

"The Bureau of Navigation has designated you six to escort the merchant vessel *Julia Luckenbach* to France and to defend her against U-boats in the most dangerous waters of the war zone. She carries a cargo of aviation parts desperately needed by the Allies. She could not be sent with the last regular convoy from here because she lost her rudder. There are no docking facilities in the Azores to handle such a repair. She will steer by towing a tug. They are standing by awaiting escort protection. I hate like hell to lose you boys because I consider you among the most competent of this group. Johnson is the senior officer. He will command."

He read the dispatch that directed the *Luckenbach* to proceed with tug and escort to Belle Isle on the coast of France, there to rendezvous with a destroyer that would relieve the escort and deliver the ship and tug to Bordeaux.

Johnson asked, "What speed will she make, sir?"

"Ten knots, I believe. I've sent for her captain. We'll find out."

"That will require us to use three engines to maintain station. At that speed our fuel will be used up the first 500 miles. I doubt if the tug can hold the ship on a straight course. She will probably cover many more miles than the actual distance to destination, which is something like 1,600 miles. My question, sir, is where do we fuel? At ten knots each chaser will burn at least 4,000 gallons of gas for the passage. Our maximum tank capacity is 2,500 gallons."

"Good question. I asked Admiral Dunn, the senior representative of the United States Navy in Ponta for a tanker to meet you half-way across. None available. Besides he thought a refueling operation in those waters would be an open invitation to attack by enemy submarines. Any of you boys have any ideas?"

I put in my two bits worth. "Sir, a fifty-gallon drum of gasoline floats because of the difference in specific gravity of gasoline and seawater. If the *Luckenbach* carries a deck cargo of drums, she can push overboard, say, ten drums at a time as requested by the chaser whose turn it is to fuel. That chaser would drop out of position, fish the drums aboard, and overtake the formation."

"How would you propose to fish them out?"

"The lowest freeboard is abeam of the davit used for handling depth charges from the magazine with chine hooks. I think we

66

could lay alongside, one drum at a time, and have a man slip the hooks over the ends of the drum. Enough men could tail on the davit falls to hoist it to the deck. It could then be immediately upended and lashed securely for pumping the gasoline to the tanks by hose."

Details of this suggestion were discussed. Eventually all were in agreement that the plan would work.

Then the captain of the *Luckenbach* appeared and upset the apple-cart. He flatly refused to carry an inflammable cargo on deck in the war zone. He said he would resign rather than subject his ship and cargo to such a hazard. He was still unpersuaded when Captain Nelson sent us back to our ships to prepare for sea.

What Captain Nelson said to him I don't know, but he capitulated, for when we departed the next morning with full tanks the *Luckenbach* carried a deck cargo of 160 drums of gasoline lashed along the rails.

Outward bound we passed a new detachment of chasers approaching the harbor. I supposed they carried our mail from Bermuda, which we had no way of collecting.

Our steaming formation was three chasers on each side of the *Luckenbach*, two ahead, one on each beam, and one on each flank. The forward positions were hazardous because the heavily laden merchant ship yawed all over the ocean. The tug, as expected, could not keep it on a straight course. At night we ran blacked out. All too often the leading chasers saw that great steel cliff of a bow bearing down on them and had to scuttle clear.

Johnson decided we no longer needed practice in manual signalling. Communications between the chasers would be by our hitherto little used radio telephones. These primitive sets were supplied primarily for tactical purposes in submarine hunting. Their useful range varied with atmospheric conditions from a maximum of twenty miles down to five. Radio operators in other ships who had never heard anything but dots and dashes were considerably startled the first time they heard voices in their headphones.

The fueling system worked, but we found we had to have relatively good weather to pick up the drums, so we filled tanks whenever such opportunity offered. In spite of the crew becoming dextrous the operation took more time than we had anticipated. The chaser that had dropped back found itself, before completing the pickup, uncomfortably lonesome on an empty and hostile ocean, the formation having long since disappeared over the horizon. On the entire passage, thanks to skillful manhandling of the heavy drums, no injuries were reported.

Eventually, on a black night, the sea flat calm, our armada stopped close to the shore of Belle Isle to await the arrival of the destroyer. The chasers drifted silent, their underwater listening devices manned, alert to the possibility of an enemy submarine finding a sitting target.

Presently the voice of the hydrophone watch came up the voice tube, "Propeller sounds bearing zero six zero relative, getting louder. Sounds like a destroyer, sir."

"Roger." The other chasers, too, were reporting to Johnson in *No. 226* by radio phone. Relative bearings were converted to magnetic. All estimates agreed that this was a destroyer approaching. The sounds ceased as she stopped engines to approach the *Luckenbach* within megaphone range, suddenly emerging out of the night, a long, slim shape completely blacked out.

A voice from a bull horn came from the destroyer's bridge, "Commanding officer of escort please identify yourself."

Johnson's voice replied, "Lieutenant Johnson, United States Navy, in U.S. *Subchaser No. 226.* Here, sir."

"You are relieved. Carry out your orders."

"We have no further orders, sir."

"Very well. I have received no orders for you. Suggest you return to the Azores."

"We have been fueling from the *Luckenbach* and her supply is exhausted. We shall have to proceed to the nearest port where we can get gasoline."

"Suggest you proceed to Brest which is under control of the United States Navy. They have a destroyer program there and some converted steam yachts but I doubt if you can get gasoline. It is all allocated to the fly-fly boys. By the way, have you had any recent enemy contacts?"

"Negative, sir. Have had none between the Azores and here."

There was a long pause, "You will. Good luck and good night." Presently the destroyer, the *Luckenbach* and the tug disappeared silently into the night.

By telephone Johnson ordered the chasers to come close enough to *No. 226* to converse over the rail.

Our position was more alarming than just shortage of fuel. Enemy submarines prowled the French coast off ports where there was a concentration of valuable targets. The only chart of the French coast we could draw at Ponta was a small scale affair covering from North Cape to Gibraltar with no harbor soundings given. It did not occur to us that lack of recognition signals might be fatal. The motto in the war zone we discovered was shoot first and inquire afterwards. These signals were changed at irregular intervals. None had been issued to us. It also occurred to me that the silhouette of a subchaser, with its low freeboard, pilot house amidships, and deck gun forward, looked uncommonly like a surfaced submarine.

In these high latitudes in May the hours of darkness were short, from 2200 to 0400 hours. The distance from Belle Isle to Brest was approximately one hundred fifteen nautical miles. Cruising on one engine to conserve our remaining fuel we could make the run in fifteen hours. *No. 143* reported fuel for a maximum of seventeen hours. This was cutting it pretty fine; actually we had no choice but to try for Brest. None of the others had fuel for more than eighteen hours.

After comparing figures and eliminating alternatives, Johnson gave the order to proceed to Brest at eight knots. We departed Belle Isle at daybreak in column led by *No. 226*, estimated time of arrival Brest 1900 hours, if nobody ran out of gas.

In retrospect, I consider it a major blunder of the Navy to order six subchasers on a mission that when completed left them without further orders or fueling facilities. There seemed to be no realization among higher echelons of the facts of life where the subchasers were concerned. At Belle Isle we were definitely "up the creek without oars." This limited understanding prevailed until major subchaser operating bases were established at Corfu and at Plymouth.

The weather was calm and hazy. The course laid by Johnson along the coast was from point to point, both because this was the shortest distance and because it afforded a check on position. At no time were we more than ten miles offshore. The first leg was a stretch of seventy nautical miles to Penmarche Pointe. Here we were fired on by a French shore battery. As the range was maximum for their guns and the gunnery poor, no hits were registered. Our only identification was the American flag flying from the antenna mast aft. What they evidently thought they saw was a column of enemy submarines on the surface.

In the afternoon four flying boats bearing British markings came toward us at low altitude. They evidently had the same idea. At the time, we were off the Pointe de Raz in water shallower than any self-respecting submarine would dare use. In spite of our inability to reply to their original challenge, they sheered off without attacking. Maybe they recognized the United States flag or concluded we were a new type of friendly patrol craft — which is exactly what we were.

The Rade de Brest, one of the finest protected anchorages in the world, is five miles wide and offers no navigational hazards for even the deepest draft ships. On the south side is a hilly promontory, on the north the city of Brest on a steep hillside. Along its waterfront an inner harbor with a narrow entrance had been artificially created by a long breakwater. This was the Port du Commerce, its many piers protected in all weathers.

Ships at anchor in the outer harbor awaiting their turn moved to the piers only to discharge or load cargos. Here also were berthed pilot boats, running boats, tugs, water tankers, and the personnel lighters that served the troop transports. All this activity was under the control of a port director. One pier housed him and his busy staff of United States Coast Guard personnel.

The overall command of naval operations had been transferred by the French to the United States Navy in the person of Rear Admiral H. B. Wilson, USN, whose operations were conducted from an office in the city which overlooked the harbor.

This was the panorama that met our eyes when Johnson led his little column into Rade de Brest where some two hundred ships then lay at anchor. From our eye-level they looked like a continuous wall of steel.

The sun at 2000 hours was still well above the western horizon. In the Port du Commerce we found the covered pier that flew an American flag and bore the sign "Port Director." We had barely enough gas remaining to run the generators for another twenty-four hours. Johnson went to the office to report our arrival and to inquire about food, water, and fuel. On his return he called the five skippers to *No. 226* for a conference. He looked tired and discouraged.

Uppermost in our minds was shortage of supplies and that none of us had received pay or mail since leaving Bermuda. Mail we could not expect; it had undoubtedly been forwarded to the Adriatic whence we had been bound when detached at the Azores. Our pay records had been handed back to each chaser by *Leonidas*, but who would take them up, and where could the crew replace much needed clothing lost in the laundry fire?

Johnson was a good officer, brief and specific. He was obviously disturbed. "Well, gentlemen," he began, "here we are, still out in left field, God's forgotten children. The duty officer here to whom I reported our arrival phoned the information to his opposite number in Operations at Headquarters. That character officially logged our arrival. He said, 'What the hell are subchasers? Never heard of them. Tell them we are running a destroyer program here and have received no orders concerning them. Tie them up to one of the buoys and don't bother me.'

"Water is no problem, we can take the hose right off the dock here. There is as yet no Navy commissary for supplies or ship's service. It will take some persuading to get the overworked disbursing office to take up our pay accounts. Our Coast guard friend commiserated. He suggested we try to beg some food for the starving American sailors from any destroyers in port. 'They are good guys,' he added.

"I have saved the worst for last. The Navy operates no aircraft out of Brest, nor any craft powered with gas engines. Even the running boats are diesel powered, consequently the Navy as yet has no gasoline supply. Our Coast Guard friend contributed the information that a British flying boat squadron operated from a base at a little place called Le Conquet. It is only a few miles overland from here. He has heard they have plenty of aviation gas. They might be persuaded to spare some. Gasoline is our first priority. Tomorrow morning Atwood and Moffat will wangle wheels from the Coast Guard and pay a call on the British. Make as an excuse our gratitude for their good judgment in deciding not to wipe us off the ocean this afternoon. Morse and Ball organize a begging operation among the destroyers and large yachts. Any food will be welcome. Phillips, you go find out about port liberty regulations before any men are allowed ashore. Tomorrow morning we move to a buoy. Any questions?"

The next morning in a Coast Guard pickup truck, George and

I arrived at the British station. This consisted of a small group of buildings and a large hangar located in a fenced area on the shelving beach of a protected cove. A marine railway for moving the flying boats to shop facilities led from water's edge into the hangar. At floats alongside a small pier, lay a couple of tenders. Four flying boats lay at mooring buoys in the cove.

Inquiries led us to the commanding officer, a pleasantly informal lieutenant, Royal Navy Volunteer Reserve, whom we found at a table in the officers' wardroom. He and three officers with him rose to greet us.

"Sit down, sit down. This is a most pleasant surprise. First things first. Steward!" He motioned us to chairs. "We were just about to have our elevenses. You'll join us in a pink gin, I hope." Introductions were completed and pink gins were produced all around.

"You must be the chaps we saw off Pointe de Raz yesterday. Must say you do look uncommonly like U-boats, from the air that is."

"We came to thank you for not blowing us out of the water. We were arriving from Ponta. Nobody had thought to issue us recognition signals so we could not answer you. We were diverted from proceeding to Gib as originally ordered and no large scale charts of this coast were available. This is our first time in the war zone."

"No U-boat will enter water too shallow to conceal him when he is on the bottom."

"We were shot with luck and you used good judgment, for which we offer both official and personal thanks."

"Well, anyway, cheers!" He raised his glass. "And welcome to the Hun's happy hunting ground. What can we do for you?"

We unfolded the inability of the United States Navy at Brest to furnish gasoline and the dire need of six subchasers unable to operate further and in a short time to be faced without even electricity. We said we had been told that this station might spare us some aviation gas. We had no idea of the international protocol involved, or how the Royal Navy would be reimbursed. Could they spare some?

"I say, you are in a bit of a spot. How much do you need?"

"It will take 15,000 gallons to fill six chasers, but anything to keep us going will be gratefully accepted."

72

"Drying out . . . ," Bermuda, 1918

"Normal roll 20°"

"We have not been too busy lately. Our boats burn a lot more gasoline than you do. We have an allowance here of 50,000 gallons a month. I think we can spare you ten thousand gallons. Our supply officer will have to cope with your people about payment."

George and I looked at each other. Whether we were more dumbfounded or grateful at this prompt response would be hard to say.

Before we could find words, our host continued. "There is one little problem—this gasoline is issued to us in cans, five imperial gallons to the can. This means transporting 2,000 cans from our warehouse by land to your ships. You can't bring them in here. Even with your shoal draft the waters inside Ushant are practically nonnavigable. Uncharted rocks and shoals all over the place. No, the cans will have to be trucked to Brest. Have another pink gin while I think."

Two pink gins later, he slapped the table. "I have it! That is, if you gentlemen can raise a few hundred francs."

I thought of the bank draft for five hundred dollars that was a parting gift from my grandfather, for, he said, emergencies. If this wasn't an emergency I didn't know what was.

"Yes," I said. "Can do. What is your plan?"

"We have one five-ton lorry here we can use. Maybe you can borrow something bigger than that pickup truck from the Navy. It is slave labor we need." He snapped his fingers. "We'll use P.O.W.'s from the prison camp outside Brest. The French troops that guard the Huns will do anything for chocolate. For chocolate and cigarettes the guards will produce enough prisoners to handle cans at both ends—and stand over them while they do it. You will have to arrange for your boats to be alongside a pier, admit prisoners to the premises, and buy cigarettes and chocolates for the guards." Thus it was arranged and carried out.

After we returned from the British base, Connolly and I decided to give half the crew shore liberty from 1600 hours to midnight, the other half the next night. None of the men had any money; they had spent the last of their pay before leaving Bermuda. I had a small supply of dollars hidden away, so I decided to make a personal loan to each man, enough to buy something to eat and a few drinks. The franc was then worth twenty-five cents. I sent Connolly to the Coast Guard office on the dock with my dollars to change into francs. This allowed me to advance each man twenty francs, the equivalent of five dollars.

The liberty regulations for the Navy were simple: keep out of any disturbances, keep out of the posted red light district, and obey the Shore Patrol. These I announced to the liberty party at muster and added a few words of my own.

"I have a kid brother who is a corporal in a famous cavalry regiment in New York City called Squadron A. When this war started the squadron was ordered to active duty. Volunteers were sought who spoke French for immediate duty in France. My brother, with visions of exciting intelligence duty, volunteered. Let this be a lesson to you—never volunteer for anything. He and five buddies found themselves in Bordeaux assigned to the Military Police, specifically to drive United States service men out of the red light district. He is disillusioned. Some of the information he has written me I am passing on to you.

"So many Frenchmen have been killed or are away at the front that there is in France today a surplus of women, all of them lonesome, many impoverished and hungry for men. They will do anything for two luxuries they are unable to get, toilet paper and soap. They know that the Navy issues safes to enlisted men on liberty, which removes an anxiety in taking Navy men to bed.

"It is not my business to know how many of you will go with a woman tonight. You don't need to speak French. The language is universal. It is my business to keep you out of trouble, such as being rolled and robbed, or contracting a venereal disease. Wherever you go, travel in pairs. Never let your buddy out of your sight. The woman who picks you up will not mind having you both in bed with her at the same time, in fact she will enjoy it. You can probably pay for her favors with a couple of cakes of soap instead of francs. The only French you need is '*Je n'ai pas de francs, mais ici c'est du savon,*' and show her soap. I advise you not to drink anything except in public in a cafe or bar. Now I am issuing you, courtesy of the United States Navy, a packet of safes and six cakes of toilet soap each. Also, here is a personal loan to be repaid to me next payday, if we ever have one, of twenty French francs each—the equivalent of five dollars—and I hope you all have an instructive evening. Be back aboard by midnight regardless. I remember an old adage which may make you popular, 'Treat a lady like a whore, and a whore like a lady.' Dismiss."

75

I decided to take a look at the city of Brest and get a bite to eat ashore for a change. As I could not raise any company I went up the hill alone to the main thoroughfare, a crowded, busy street of shops and sidewalk cafes doing a thriving business in the late afternoon sunshine. There were many American uniforms, both Army and Navy, among the French. A large transport had arrived that morning from the United States with a couple of thousand troops.

It was a complete surprise to come face to face with a close friend and neighbor from Flushing looking very smart in the uniform of a captain of artillery. I knew that he had enrolled in the Army Reserve but had no idea that his outfit was one that had arrived that morning. Figuratively we fell on each other's necks and in two minutes were sitting at a sidewalk table with aperitifs on the way. Stanley Reinhart was a bachelor, one of Sally's many devotees who was always welcome in our house. I knew he would have late word of her.

"Tell me all about Sally and the kids," I blurted. "No mail has reached us since we left Bermuda nearly six weeks ago. Just as we left we passed the ship coming in from New York that carried mail, but no way of connecting with it. Name is *Charibdis*."

"Then you didn't know Sally was on that ship, coming down to visit you in Bermuda. Your grandfather blew her to the trip. She guessed from your letters that you were where you had spent your honeymoon and took a chance that you would not have gone."

I just stared at him. "Oh, no!" was all I could say.

"It was a pretty tough disappointment for her, but she is back home safe and sound after a pretty hairy six days in Bermuda fighting off the wolves before she could leave. You must admit that a young married woman without a husband is a challenge to every unattached officer in sight, particularly if she looks like your Sally. But she is still your Sally, all right, and always will be I guess."

"When did you last see her?"

"Ten days ago, just before we embarked. Leslie and I took her to the Century Roof for dinner and heard all about her adventures."

So we dined and wined while like a sponge I soaked up all the information he could give me about Sally and the children and finally about my family and friends. When I returned to *No. 143* I sat up for two hours writing a heartfelt love letter.

Twenty-four hours after our visit to the British base, each

chaser had taken on 2,000 imperial gallons and was back at the buoy.

Morse and Ball had been well received by destroyers and yachts alike and we were now fairly well provisioned with staples and fresh meat. They also brought back interesting information about enemy activities in the Bay of Biscay where many merchant vessels had been torpedoed — particularly by one submarine whose skipper had been dubbed "Penmarche Pete" because he so often operated in the vicinity of Penmarche Pointe.

Pete's submarine was equipped with radio telephone over which he talked volubly in excellent English. He said that he had been a shipmaster in the United States for ten years and happened to be in Germany when war broke out. Being German born, he joined the Imperial Navy, trained for the submarine service, and was eventually given this command with the rank of Kapitan-zur-See. Unlike more ruthless submarine skippers he seemed to regard sinking merchant tonnage as a sort of sporting venture. He always gave his victims time to abandon ship, was never known to fire on a lifeboat, and on one occasion towed a string of lifeboats to within sight of land.

The commanding officer of one of the destroyers working out of Brest was Lieutenant Commander Taussig. Pete liked to bedevil him because of his German name; told him he ought to be in the Imperial Navy. One time when Taussig had an evening ashore in Bordeaux he dined at a popular restaurant. The next day Pete called the destroyer to tell Taussig he was sorry the exigencies of war prevented his joining him at his table. He then proceeded to itemize what Taussig had had for dinner, indicating that he too had been ashore in Bordeaux that night, wearing a French uniform, probably in the company of a German agent, not an impossible visit for a daring man put ashore by appointment in a rubber boat.

A week later, still without pay, mail, or replacement of underclothes for the crew, orders were received dated May 9, 1918, to proceed to England.

Chapter 7

Brest to England — Headquarters London

THE ORDERS were signed by Rear Admiral H. B. Wilson, commanding United States Naval Forces in France. We were to proceed to Portsmouth, England, there to report to the commanding officer of the USS *Aylwin* for duty. Before departure we were to familiarize ourselves with positions of enemy minefields and submarines as shown on the board in the operations room. An attached sheet showed conditions in the English Channel, and which channels on the French coast were closed and which open. Full communications instructions were set forth. At last we had recognition signals.

The rest of the day was spent in preparations for sea. The bread available in Brest was dark gray in color and gritty in texture. Connolly made a deal with a small bakery in the city to bake white bread for us from Navy flour. In payment the baker was to keep for his own use half the flour delivered to him. Thus one hundred pounds of flour was converted into delectable, fresh French loaves of white bread that the crew brought aboard that afternoon. The baker was the happiest man in France. He said he had not been able to make good bread since the war started.

Johnson headed our visit to Operations, thoroughly to familiarize ourselves with the master chart on which all current information about the enemy was plotted. On returning we met aboard *No. 226* to discuss what we had seen and to receive Johnson's sailing instructions. The distance from Brest to Portsmouth is approximately 270 nautical miles, twenty-seven running hours at ten knots. The twenty-three-foot rise and fall of tide in the English Channel creates a current of two to four knots depending on whether the wind is with or against it. In twenty-seven hours the current would be favoring us for a period about equal to the time it would be against us.

Johnson decided to depart at 0900 hours the next morning, which would make our ETA (estimated time of arrival), if not slowed by head seas, about 1200 hours the following day, May 11. Our landfall was to be the Isle of Wight outside Southampton water where Portsmouth was located. Formation in column, fifty yards between chasers. If fog was encountered we were to close up to echelon, each chaser moving up on the port quarter of the next ahead to stay within visual distance. At night the shielded blue stern light was to guide the next astern, otherwise the ships were to be completely blacked out. Radio telephones were to be manned at all times for intership communication. Depth charges on the racks were to be set alternately for fifty and for one hundred feet; the two Y-gun charges for fifty feet. The three-inch gun forward and the machine guns on the bridge were to be loaded, also ready ammunition carried on deck. Speed ten knots on two wing engines.

This plan of operation was good because it afforded spare time to reach Portsmouth before dark.

We were all aware that for the first time we were entering waters where enemy attack could occur at any moment, our first operation with depth charges armed and guns ready for action. We had been informed by the briefing officer at Brest Operations that an attack by an enemy submarine would be on the surface by gunfire. For two reasons, he said, the Germans would not attack us by torpedo: first because their torpedos were too expensive and too precious to waste on small fry, and second because their depth setting control was unreliable if set to run shallow enough to hit us. A normal depth setting would pass harmlessly beneath our keels.

In spite of this reassurance, I know that on that beautiful May morning we all felt an unexpected tension as we set forth. We could not forget that a U-boat's deck gun could outrange ours by two thousand yards.

When darkness fell the sea was still calm and we had checked our position by a lighthouse, dark for the duration, on the Casquets, a group of rocky islets. What shipping we saw was at a distance. Shortly before midnight fog providentially shut in and we became more concerned with keeping close echelon formation than with the possibility of enemy attack. Our course kept us well south of the travelled shipping lines, which minimized the hazard of collision.

When the sun was up the next morning a light breeze came in from the northeast. This we later found to be the Channel's fair weather sector. The fog soon dispelled. At 1300 hours with a fair tide under us we sighted St. Catherine's lighthouse on the Isle of Wight.

Three hours later we berthed at the British Naval Dockyard at Portsmouth, passage uneventfully completed. Hauled out high on a marine railway nearby was a destroyer flying the stars and stripes. This was USS *Aylwin*, our destination.

We six subchaser skippers, shaved and shined in our best uniforms, climbed a tall ladder to the *Aylwin*'s deck, there to be met by a Negro chief steward's mate, the only crew member in sight.

"Come aboard, gen'lmen," he said hospitably, returning our salutes, "Cap'n LeBreton he ain't aboard right now, but I expec' him back shortly. If you all will make yo'selves comfortable in the wardroom I'll fetch coffee."

While we drank coffee and waited we saw no officers or crew, all apparently ashore, although a number of dockyard workers were busily engaged at various jobs.

Our host evidently had a high regard for his captain for he regaled us with many stories of his accomplishments. From his post by the wardroom door he kept the ladder under observation.

"Here he come, now," he said rushing to the gangway. We rose to await the great man's entrance.

He entered lugging a heavy golf bag, appropriately wearing plus-fours, a loud sport shirt, and a golf cap with brim canted well over one eye to conceal a beautiful shiner. If not exactly what we expected, he was, nevertheless, an impressive figure of a man.

"Well, well," he said, dumping his golf bag, "welcome aboard. I wondered when you'd arrive. I'm Lieutenant Commander David LeBreton, skipper of this bucket. I hope Sam has been taking good care of you." We introduced ourselves.

Our orders to report for duty to the *Aylwin* had stimulated considerable speculation among the chasers as to the nature of the duty. Ten-knot chasers operating with a thirty-knot destroyer did not somehow seem practical. Commander LeBreton's next statement came as a surprise.

80

"Orders for you arrived by guard mail yesterday signed by Admiral Sims himself. They are dated May 9. You six commanding officers are to leave your ships here in charge of your executive officers, proceed to Headquarters in London, and there report to the commander United States Naval Forces Operating in European Waters for special temporary duty.

"On completion of the temporary duty you will resume present duty, which means in command of your respective ships. By this I assume that in London you will be under instruction for operations for which you will receive later orders." He produced a sheaf of papers. "The interesting thing about these orders is that they are issued to each of you individually and not as a division."

The orders were distributed to us. They included instructions in regard to expenses.

Johnson asked, "When do we depart for London, sir? These orders say when in your opinion our duties permit."

"I'd say that was when you tell me the activities of your crews in your absence have been planned with your executive officers and temporary command transferred. Report to me when you are ready to leave your ships. If you can get ready in time I would suggest that tomorrow you take the night train to London, which would get you there about 0600 hours. That will give you time to stop off in the hotel in the terminal to wash up and shave and get breakfast before reporting. Headquarters opens at 0800 hours. If that is agreeable I'll phone the Chief of Staff to expect you at that time the day after tomorrow."

Johnson answered for all of us, "Can do, sir. I believe we have no repairs to be made that can't be handled by our own men. However, the ships should be fueled before we leave them. Where do we get gasoline?"

"The British have been very cooperative. I expected you would need gasoline. They maintain a large supply at their CMB base just across the harbor. You can see it from here. The pier is narrow and only a couple of hundred feet long. You will have to take on fuel there one at a time on the east side of the pier because their marine railway is on a sloping beach close to the west side. We have twenty-three-foot rise and fall of tide here, but even at low water you will have enough depth alongside. I have arranged for you to sign for your gas. They must have quite a supply; I am told a CMB burns 50 gallons an hour on each engine. Their PLE [patrol limit of endurance] is said to be six hours."

I stuck my neck out to ask the question we were all dying to ask but didn't want to betray our ignorance, "Just what is a CMB, sir?"

"No reason you should know, because it has been pretty much hush-hush. A CMB is a coastal motorboat, a fifty-foot hydroplane, and it has proved to be an effective weapon for hit-and-run raids on enemy held ports in Belgium. It carries two twenty-one-inch torpedoes; fully armed and fueled it has a cruising speed of fifty knots and is controlled by a single officer strapped into a bucket seat on deck. Another man, located below, watches the engines and handles the radio. They are driven by a pair of twelve-cylinder Rolls-Royce or Green aviation engines. The wooden hull is almost tubular in section, very light, very strong with flat canoe ribs and three diagonal layers of thin planking glued together. When not engaged on a mission they are kept hauled out under cover. I may add that this service is manned by Royal Navy Volunteer Reserves, who are a bunch of young daredevils, most of them professional race drivers, stunt men, and the like. During the last year fatalities have run about fifty per cent. You will meet some characters over there! I'll phone them to expect you."

We told Captain LeBreton that we had found nobody to take up our pay accounts since leaving Bermuda. He said, "Bad for morale for the men to have nothing to spend ashore. You get your pay accounts over here to my paymaster. I'll instruct him to carry them until further orders and to make up an immediate payroll covering all back pay for officers and men. You will be paid in pounds, shillings, and pence, of course."

We expressed fervent gratitude.

After a few more questions and answers we returned to our ships. Johnson ordered *No. 143* to proceed to the CMB base at 0600 hours the next morning.

A group of CMB officers were on the pier when we approached gingerly because of low tide. The railing on top of our pilot house was just level with the surface of the pier. They were a merry bunch, all bearded, dressed in a weird assortment of garments but wearing officers' caps. They ceased their horseplay and repartee to take our lines, studying us curiously from above.

82

I thanked them and asked them to come aboard to look us over and have a cup of coffee. One of them found a ten-foot plank two inches thick but only about eight inches wide that bridged the space between the stringpiece of the pier to the railing on top of our pilot house. The first man walked cautiously across imitating a tightrope walker. The second made the gestures of a ballerina in an imaginary ballet skirt, pausing on the way to blow kisses to the audience. The next man hesitated a minute, then sat down straddling the board. I heard him murmur, "And what did you do in the great war, daddy?—Hush, my child, I crawled."

It was a cordial visit on both sides, interrupted by the distant sound of high speed engines. All hands lined the deck as the sound approached from the other side of a point. Simultaneously a car with a padded cradle rumbled down the railway into the water ready to take a CMB.

One of the Britishers remarked, "Old Freddy made it! Good show!" He turned to me, "It is so calm this morning he thought he'd have a go at Dunkirk. That's just about as far as these boats can go and get back again. They make a bit better speed after they get rid of the weight of torpedoes and half their gas. Evidently had no engine trouble. They sound sweet, don't they?"

Moments later the CMB raced around the point at top speed. Everyone gasped. A third of her bow was shot away, the engines visible in the open end of the hull travelling only inches clear of the surface. As it swept toward the pier without slackening speed it narrowly bypassed the half-submerged cradle, hit the beach, and skidded two boat lengths high and dry ashore in a flurry of sand scooped into the open end of the hull. At the moment of impact the pilot cut the engines. Propellers, shafts, struts, and rudders were buried in the beach in a tangle of wreckage that braked the boat to a halt.

The radio man stood in an open hatch. The pilot unstrapped himself from his control seat and stood up, removing a crash helmet. He was a tall, skinny young man with flaming red hair and beard, wearing a padded life jacket. He waved gaily to the crowd lining No. 143's rail. "It's been a long, hard day mates," he called. "How about joining me for a spot in the wardroom. You two Yanks come along, too." Old Freddy had been alone at the wheel since the first crack of daylight running at fantastic speed. He had obviously been in action and equally obviously had barely escaped death. I was suddenly overwhelmingly aware that the enemy we so casually talked about was very real. As Connolly and I followed the group toward the wardroom, I felt an unaccustomed sensation in my stomach.

Dancy supervised the refueling while we, over a warm Scotch and soda, listened to Old Freddy's account of his morning's mission, as laconic and understated a report as only a Britisher could be capable of.

The month of May produces more days of flat calm in the English Channel than any other month. Only such a day enabled the CMB to try to reach Dunkirk in the hope of finding one of the German E-boats. These were fast, heavily armed patrol boats about the size of a United States subchaser, but deep enough to be vulnerable to torpedo attack. Old Freddy casually mentioned that information about the location of enemy minefields appeared to be accurate, that the mines were set at least ten feet below the surface. He decided that on full plane at fifty knots he could pass over them, which he did. Dunkirk is a small harbor with a pier at which he spotted an E-boat. He lined his CBM up for a perfect broadside torpedo shot and did not release a torpedo until he was within 500 yards.

In Old Freddy's words, "After I hit the button the fish missed my stern by at least five feet. There was a lovely boom and the E-boat simply disintegrated. Unfortunately, a gun that I had not spotted on the end of the pier opened up. I had to get end on to give them the smallest target area, so as I still had my other torpedo I decided to head toward the pierhead instead of away. Damned silly of me as it turned out. The shot that knocked the bow off was fired just after I hit the button. At least I blew the end off the pier and had the satisfaction of seeing the gun and the gun crew fly forty feet in the air. Then the only problem was to get home without sinking. Thanks to the weather here we are. Sorry to have creamed the boat. Next time I will try not to be such a bloody fool."

The orders to proceed to London were dated May 9. We were handed them in Portsmouth two days later and on May 12 turned the six chasers over to our executive officers, fueled and operative, and caught the night train to London. Promptly at 0800 hours the next morning we presented ourselves at the imposing old building on Grosvenor Square that housed United States Navy Headquarters.

We were surprised and impressed to be accorded the boarding

honors of commanding officers notwithstanding our very junior ranks. Six sideboys stood to attention as we entered to be greeted by a senior captain who returned our salutes and introduced himself as the chief of staff. He welcomed us warmly and identified us by name in order to introduce us individually to Admiral Sims who had asked to see us on arrival.

Vice Admiral William Sims, USN, Commander United States Naval Forces in Europe, rose from his chair at a vast, completely empty desk to greet us. He was tall, slender, and erect, with thinning white hair and a pointed white beard, his ruddy face dominated by twinkling blue eyes and a half-smile. He told us we were here to learn all that Operations could teach us about the enemy and to learn the measures being taken by the navies of the Allies to combat enemy operations in order to safeguard the passage of shipping. He said we would be under the tuition of a group of senior operations watch officers of our Navy, the Royal Navy, and the French Navy, who were trained intelligence officers. When they reported they had imparted to us all the information they could, we were to be brought back to him for orders and a final briefing. Our impression of the admiral was that he was a man of great simplicity combined with quiet authority, a dedicated leader of men.

In the center of the operations room was an immense chart table portraying an area that included the Bay of Biscay, the English Channel, the North Sea, the Irish Sea, and the Atlantic to longitude 20° west. On this table were small markers of different colors moved by long handled pushers to the latest known or estimated positions of enemy and Allied forces. Positions were updated as dispatches were received from the adjacent communications room. Allied defensive minefields were delineated by crayon, as were reported or suspected German mined areas. Blackboards and clipboards on the walls carried classified information for ready reference.

The atmosphere in this busy room was informal and relaxed. The officers on duty were in their shirt sleeves, most of them smoking. Small groups discussed dispatches brought in by uniformed messengers. Here we were turned over to the senior watch officer for introductions all around, and each assigned to a duty officer. These officers were particularly interested to learn about the capabilities and limitations of the subchasers, a new arm of the Navy about which they were completely uninformed.

In this room we spent most of the next forty-eight hours, taking time out only to snatch a little sleep in a room equipped with a few cots, to shave, and to eat.

On our third night at Operations when the Chief of Staff came in to inspect, he suggested that a night's sleep would be good for the chaser officers. He had had reserved for us three double rooms at a nearby hotel. It was now 2200 hours. He would expect us back at 0800 the next morning. Six weary junior officers were headed for bed before you could say knife.

George and I elected to share a room. It was an old hotel as quiet as a tomb, with Victorian furnishings and no elevator. All windows were blacked out with curtains. The personable young woman who tended the switchboard doubled as desk clerk. She handed us keys to rooms in different parts of the hotel and directed George and me to ours on the second floor. "I'll be off duty at midnight," she said, looking squarely at George.

I was so sound asleep I did not hear her enter. I was startled awake by my bed covers being pulled down when she sat on the edge of the bed. Her hair fell over my face and her robe hung open when she leaned over to kiss me. I was ashamed to feel a wave of sheer lust as I pushed away her inquisitive hand.

"You want George in the other bed over there. He is the great stud of our outfit," I said thickly.

The other bed was across the room. "What goes on?" said George.

"You appear to have a caller."

"Well, well. I was just dreaming that something nice would happen. Send her over. I'm ready."

So I had to lie there and listen in a tumult of emotion while George expertly justified his reputation.

On her way out she paused at my bed. "Change your mind?" she said laughing, "I'm ready if you are." Silently the door closed behind her.

"These English nymphos," said George, "I've heard about them. They are as advertised! Sorry to disturb your sleep. Good night."

On the afternoon of May 13 we received our briefing from Admiral Sims. The written orders we received were simply a second endorsement of the orders that brought us to London. "Temporary Duty completed this date." These orders returned us to duty under

86

the commanding officer of USS *Aylwin*. Accordingly, we were highly interested to learn what the admiral had to say.

He spoke standing, "Gentlemen, I am informed that you have reacted intelligently to the information you have been asked to absorb in a brief period and that you have furnished us most helpful information about the subchasers. I would like to give you orders consisting of only five words, 'Close probable position enemy submarines!' However, as logistics make such orders impractical, I have discussed by telephone with Captain LeBreton your deployment until such time as Subchaser Base No. 27 is ready at Plymouth. We hope the new base will be operative early in July. Until then we have decided that you will operate out of the port of Weymouth engaged in antisubmarine patrol. We selected Weymouth because of its proximity to the Royal Dockyard at Portland from which you can obtain repairs and depth charges, but principally because Weymouth is an active ML [motor launch] base. The MLs, as you know, have American Standard engines identical to yours so you will be able to draw repair parts as needed. You will organize in two units, four days and four nights at sea and four days and four nights in port on maintenance and standby. You are under the command of Captain LeBreton. You will maintain a twenty-four-hour radio watch both at sea and in port for such orders as you may receive from him. *Aylwin* will be operating in the English Channel prepared to support your operations as necessary.

"You are now organized in two units that will alternate duty at sea and in port. Unit 1 under command of Lieutenant (j.g.) Atwood comprises subchasers *No.'s 177, 143,* and *148.* Unit 2 under command of Lieutenant Johnson comprises subchasers *No.'s 226, 224,* and *351.* After you report for duty at the new subchaser base these two units will receive a division designation.

"All that I can add is to wish you good hunting." He extended a hand, "Good morning, gentlemen." We each received a firm handshake and a warm smile. After farewells in Operations we departed for the next train to Portsmouth with a broader view of the war effort, as well as an understanding of the part the subchasers were expected to play.

Chapter 8

English Channel—Weymouth—Enemy Action

WE FOUND *Aylwin* afloat at a buoy. Captain LeBreton confirmed what we had been told by Admiral Sims. He said that henceforth orders to Atwood and Johnson for their two units would be either verbal or by dispatch. He did not intend to get involved in unnecessary paper work. Our immediate orders were to prepare for sea and to proceed to Weymouth. Atwood and Johnson were to report arrival to him by dispatch, then identify ourselves to the commanding officer of the ML base. Presumably he would offer the hospitality of his pier to our off-duty unit. The unit at sea was to hunt between the Isle of Wight and the Eddystone light off Plymouth until relieved by dispatch or phone from the other unit on its arrival in the area.

Johnson elected to take the first patrol, so Unit 1 made an uneventful passage to the little port of Weymouth, a distance of only sixty-five miles, there to establish an entente cordiale with the British. The weather was fine, the visibility hazy.

The little town nestled on the east side of a high promontory called Portland Bill adjacent to His Majesty's Dockyard. This promontory extended south six miles into the English Channel, affording a lee from the prevailing westerlies. Ample harbor was formed by a breakwater protecting the anchorage from the east and south. Weymouth boasted a boardwalk reminiscent of Atlantic City on a small scale, a recreation pier, and two theatres. In addition to the dockyard facilities in the angle formed by the promontory, there was an ammunition depot with a separate loading pier, a big

88

seaplane hangar, and the facilities of the ML base. Weymouth looked to us like an ideal operating base for small craft.

We were cordially welcomed at the ML pier where we tied up. Officers and men alike showed the liveliest interest in our ships. A stream of visitors continued to come aboard, offering all kinds of helpful information, as well as the hospitality of their base facilities for both the officers and men. The enlisted personnel seemed to hit it off unexpectedly well, particularly the engine-room ratings whose lives were identified with identical engines.

The more we saw of the British and learned what they had accomplished, in their inscrutable businesslike way, in their small craft operations the higher regard we had for them. They were a modest lot, belittling living conditions in their smaller ships far more cramped than ours. Their humor, after more than two years of hazardous duty, was unquenchable. They called the MLs sea slugs. The Royal Navy dubbed them Cinderellas of the Fleet. They were all manned by the Royal Navy Volunteer Reserve.

By 1917 many of the surviving MLs were beginning to wear out. The United States Navy's 110-foot subchasers, first produced in 1917, were intended to replace them. Our two units were the first to reach an ML base. No wonder curiosity was keen!

George Atwood and I decided to hire lodgings in the town for our off-duty nights. We were directed to a Mrs. Hansfield, a dear old lady whose son had recently been killed in France. From her we rented a connecting living room and bedroom with two beds. The bay window overlooked the harbor. Mrs. Hansfield agreed to let us have this spic-and-span little apartment, do our laundry, take care of our mending, and serve us breakfasts, all for the sum of one pound per week!

Unit 1 relieved Unit 2 off Portland Bill by radio appointment on May 17. The weather continued calm, so George was able to lie close enough to *No. 226* to talk over the rail with Johnson to inform him of the cooperative atmosphere in Weymouth.

The tactical procedure for our submarine hunting was for the unit to steam in line abreast at the maximum distance between ships appropriate to the weather conditions, usually between five hundred and a thousand yards. The leader is the center ship. The officer on watch in each chaser mans the telephone in the pilot house. After an arbitrary distance has been run, the leader gives three successive commands, each of which is acknowledged by the other two: "Standby," "Stop," and "Down Tubes." At the order "Stop" all engines and auxiliary machinery are simultaneously stopped. As soon as the chaser has lost enough way to reduce water noises, the hydrophone operator lowers a listening device called a C-tube. This is a pipe structure in the shape of an inverted T, in effect an underwater stethoscope. The vertical member passes through a stuffing box to the horizontal member, which when under way is pulled up against the hull alongside the keel. Lowered to the down position it can be rotated 360° by a hand wheel on top. The operator wears stethoscope ear pieces connected by rubber tubes leading through the pipes to the ends of the horizontal member, which are fitted with diaphragms. When the operator detects a propeller, or other underwater sound, by rotating the hand wheel until the volume of sound is equal in both ears, he can determine the direction of the sound relative to the ship's bow. This bearing is called up a voice tube to the officer on watch. He converts this from a relative to a magnetic bearing, which he announces by phone.

The leader plots on his chart his own ship's bearing as well as the bearings reported by the other two. Where these three lines intersect is the source of the sound. Changes in bearings reported continuously by the listeners indicate the direction in which the target is moving. The leader announces a new course, the command "Up Tubes" is passed and the chasers get under way, swinging to a line at right angles to the estimated course of the target. This gives the widest possible angles to the bearings at the next stop.

A submerged sub running on electric power at slow speed makes little propeller noise, drowned out by interference from the sound of larger or higher speed propellers. The sub's escape tactics are to stop his propeller when the chasers stop, allowing only seconds for the chasers to obtain bearings. The sub continues this procedure until a larger ship passes even at a distance, which makes enough sound interference to enable him to move out of sound range of the hunters. By daylight the vessel causing interference with the hunt is usually visible, but nothing can be done about it. Thus, sub hunting becomes frustrating, largely a matter of luck if the chasers can get close enough for a depth charge attack.

Unit 1 followed these listening tactics for a day and a night, becoming proficient in making simultaneous stops and taking rapid bearings. We practiced on every vessel we could see. On May 19, the third day out, we were practicing on a destroyer that we could see approaching from the west. It proved to be American. As it was not *Aylwin*, we assumed it was either out of Queenstown or Brest where the United States Navy based destroyer operations.

To our great surprise it stopped nearby *No. 143* and put over a boat that embarked a distinguished looking officer wearing scrambled eggs on his cap and four gold stripes. With his dunnage bag he was put aboard *No. 143*. I had not the faintest idea of the protocol involved, so I took refuge in greeting him just as I would an unexpected visitor coming aboard my yacht. Connolly and I were only distinguishable from the men by our caps; all hands were in dungarees and life jackets. The ship had not had a lick of paint since Bermuda. I decided to make no apologies. I simply extended my hand and said, "Glad to have you aboard, sir. I am Ensign Moffat and this is my exec, Boatswain Connolly."

He smiled warmly, "My name is Schofield. I am very glad to be aboard. Please accept me as a guest and carry on your usual routine. My role is observer from the Bureau of Navigation in Washington. They want first-hand information as to how the subchaser program is working, so I was sent out, via Queenstown, to board at random the first chaser I met on patrol. I'll be with you until you are relieved."

The time was 1200 hours, a beautiful day, sea as calm as a lake. The first shift was below at their midday meal. "Have you had lunch, sir?" I asked after the captain had dismissed the launch. "Hope you don't mind messing with the crew. Connolly and I find it more practical. After all there are certain advantages in being close to the galley, particularly when it's rough."

I directed Florin to put the captain's bag in my berth. "Let's eat, then. If you don't mind, I'll lead the way." Captain Schofield followed me down the vertical ladder to the crew's quarters aft. In spite of the limited headroom the eight men at table tried to stand.

Captain Schofield said, "Sit down, gentlemen, please."

"Hunch over, boys," I said. "This is our guest, Captain Schofield, all the way from Washington. We'll sit each side of this end." When we were seated, I said, "Captain, I would like to introduce to you a dedicated group of civilians who are doing their best in a new environment and a new way of life. To my mind, they are doing one hell of a job. On your right is Mr. Dancy who used to run the municipal power plant at Holly Springs, Mississippi. Next to him is Mr. Webb, woodsman and linotype operator from California. Mr. Todd is a merchant marine ship's quartermaster on the Great Lakes; Mr. Grady is an electrician from Massachusetts; Mr. Smith is a cow puncher from Texas; Mr. Hayforth is a chemist from Minnesota; Mr. Scheuerman is an automobile repairman from Chicago; and the big guy smiling at you from the galley is our provider, Cook Loden. He was a sharecropper in Texas. You will meet the rest of the boys later."

If I had had a crystal ball I would have seen that this unassuming and courteous guest was later in his career, as vice admiral, to reach the highest rung in the Navy ladder, chief of Naval Operations.

Connolly and I, like the rest of the crew, stood four hours on and four off. I turned my berth over to the Captain and took turns with Connolly in his berth. I forgot that my secret listening post would be discovered. Discreetly, he did not mention it but I could tell that he had heard some revealing conversation from the crew's quarters.

My first watch the next day was 0400 to 0800 hours. The longest day in the year was only a month away. In those high latitudes dawn broke at 0400 and it was full daylight by 0430. The Captain graciously offered to stand my watch and suggested I turn in in my own berth when he relieved Connolly.

I was fathoms deep in sleep when the klaxon horn signalling general quarters brought Connolly and me to our feet. The engine room telegraphs jangled to full speed ahead. I grabbed my lifebelt and scrambled up the ladder barefoot in my underclothes. The gun crew were at their stations, the captain on top of the pilot house calling rapidly decreasing ranges to the gun pointer. I took one look at the target and yelled, "Secure from general quarters! Captain, she's British! We know that ship." Thus was averted what might have been a major blunder, if not an international incident.

The Captain climbed down from his perch, his face very red. "Thank you, Moffat. She looked like a U-boat to me. What is she?"

"An experimental submersible destroyer running trials out of Weymouth. The boys at the ML base told me to look out for her, but I forgot to warn you. She is a high speed destroyer on the surface designed to have the silhouette of a German sub. They call her a P-boat. She can make a crash dive while doing twenty knots. The rub is that with a full head of steam in the boilers, even though the fires are doused to save oxygen, the crew can't survive the temperature in the hull. Rumor is that they are about to cancel further experiments."

We exchanged recognition signals and the P-boat proceeded toward Weymouth on the surface, unaware of the sting she might have received from our little three-inch twenty-three-calibre gun.

When we were relieved by Unit 2, Captain Schofield transferred to *No. 351,* commanded by my friend Will Ball, a competent ensign who later made the Navy a career. He eventually retired as a rear admiral.

On our next patrol, after a short spell of choppy seas which we missed, we had our first enemy action. Unit 1 was operating as a bobtailed unit in the absence of *No. 148* undergoing major engine repairs. On May 30, *No.'s 177* and *143* drifted silent, fifteen miles south of St. Catherine's light, Isle of Wight, tubes down, half a mile apart in fifty fathoms. An ebbing tide carried us west at about three knots, the surface so still that the tide made dimples. Not a breath of air stirred; the horizon all around was lost in haze. The chasers seemed to exist in a vast bowl where sea merged with sky under the rays of a hot noon sun. The listener reported nothing stirring. I stood talking with Dancy at the engine-room hatch; Connolly manned the telephone in the wheelhouse; the men idled at their stations at gun and depth charges. Then, with appalling suddenness, it happened.

The listener's voice came loud and clear up the voice tube, "Chaser starting up close aboard, sir. I'll have the bearing in a moment." *No. 177* had not moved; her engines would have been audible. There was only the sound of water bubbling about three boats' lengths astern. Then emerged the conning tower and deck of a submarine, a sinister black hull twice our length surfacing stern to stern with us. Our bow gun obviously could not be brought to bear. As I raced for the bridge, Connolly hit the klaxon. I yelled to him, "All engines ahead full!" Dancy dove below; he anticipated the order. Two of the three engines were warm and started even as I gave the next orders, the only thing I could do in the circumstances. To my dismay my teeth chattered. "Drop two charges. Fire Y-gun!" The first two on the stern racks were set for fifty feet as were the two on the Y-gun. All were armed to fire. The three-inch cartridge in the Y-gun made a report that drowned the noise of the engines as two charges soared into the air, one on each side to drop a boat's length away. The sinister black monster rotated its periscope once, then withdrew it even as it started forward in a crash dive.

No. 143 had started to gain headway when the four charges detonated simultaneously. They countermined in one shattering blast that lifted our stern out of water and surged us forward with the propellers racing in the air. All hands were knocked to the deck. We were probably less than half the distance we should have covered before dropping. When I picked myself up, the conning tower of the sub was almost submerged, still moving slowly away. There was no way of telling what damage, if any, we had done. At any rate, our engines were still running. George Atwood's angry voice on the speaker yelled, "What the hell are you trying to do, dropping charges without warning! You've probably ruptured my listener's eardrums!"

I stopped the engines. My ears were still ringing. At the moment of the explosion it seemed as though the surface of the sea was an enormous pane of plate glass shattered with a splintering crash from beneath by a great hammer. Following a quivering pause, a section of ocean astern was lifted bodily in a white column of water that fell for several seconds. I felt the slap when our stern hit the surface. The pilot house was a shambles of broken glass.

Ganzenmuller's voice came up the tube, "Tube up, sir. I got it up when the engines started before we got moving. 'Guess I had the ear pieces out of my ears just in time. What happened, sir?"

"We just attacked an enemy submarine that surfaced astern of us. You did a heads-up job. Stand by for orders."

"Did we sink him?"

"That's what we'll try to find out."

I reported to George what had happened. "I think she was sitting on the bottom waiting to come up for air until she heard no propellers. We'd been stopped for at least twenty minutes and were carried down to her on the tide without her suspecting there was anyone about. If she is able to move we should be able to hear her. If she is damaged and has gone to the bottom we've got to locate her for another attack."

"Roger. You buoy the spot for a reference point where you think you made the drop. We'll make a sound search together making stops every three or four minutes. Let's go."

First *No. 177* reported hearing mechanical noises; then we too picked them up. We determined that they were not moving. I put on the ear pieces myself to try to identify them. There was an occasional definite sound of hammering, a less definite sound that may have been filing, and then a sputtering electrical noise like a shorted circuit.

We stayed in sight of the life jacket I had anchored as a marker buoy. Dancy reported we had opened up a few seams aft but nothing the pumps could not keep ahead of when we were not stopped for listening. Most of the glass portlights below the rail had cracked.

We marked on our charts the estimated location of the sub, from cross bearings on the sounds, to be about three hundred yards east of our marker on the bottom in 150 feet of water. The tide had another hour to ebb before reversing direction.

As yet the attack had not been reported. We decided to move to positions to form a triangle with the sub's position on the bottom and there anchor to await slack tide before making another attack, thus eliminating the calculation for current. Each chaser carried a full coil of manila for just such a contingency, to be cut and buoyed. The chain took too long to haul aboard.

I almost broke the heart of our single-minded cook by not allowing him to launch the wherry to retrieve enough fish for supper from the thousands brought to the surface by the explosion. I told him if he could fashion a dip net he could have all he could reach from the deck. We had fresh fish for supper.

It was while maneuvering to anchor that we first saw a spreading patch of oil which turned the surface irridescent. Allowing for the set of the tide it appeared to be coming to the surface from about the area where we believed the sub had bottomed.

We determined the predicted time of slack water at which *No. 177* would run out his bearing on the target to drop a full depth charge pattern. We would give him the word "Mark" over the phone and flash our masthead light at the instant he crossed our line of bearing. George set his charges to detonate from twenty to forty feet above bottom. He had about three hundred yards to run to the target area, so he had time to work up to his top speed before laying the pattern. This saved *No. 177* from the shaking up *No. 143* had sustained. It was a magnificent show, eight charges each carrying three hundred pounds of TNT detonating like clockwork.

George then returned to his buoyed anchor to observe results.

Among the many fish of all sizes brought up by the explosions it was impossible to spot any debris from the sub or bodies, but tons of oil spread over a large area, trailing down the tide as far as could be seen.

Then George reported the attack. Unit 1 was ordered to stay at anchor until the *Aylwin* arrived, ETA in about three hours.

Aylwin had no more luck than Unit 1 in producing evidence of a kill, in spite of dropping thirty more charges.

However, a week later a dispatch from the British Admiralty to Admiral Sims recognized the attack by two subchasers of Unit 1 and identified the German submarine by number. It stated that no further operations by this submarine were reported by Intelligence. It had not returned to port. Estimate: probably damaged. It was not until long after the war that a friend in the Admiralty sent me word that our particular sub was undoubtedly destroyed. At the end of the war it was still reported missing.

On our return to Weymouth, *No. 143* was leaking badly astern. The dockyard accomplished the necessary caulking by simply lifting the stern out of water by crane so that the caulkers could work from a float. We were again operative in time for the next patrol. While we were away, *No. 148* had been ordered to Portsmouth to be docked for underwater repairs and did not rejoin Unit 1 until six weeks later in Plymouth. *No.'s 177* and *143* continued to operate as a two-chaser unit throughout our patrols out of Weymouth.

During this period we experienced our first taste of Channel weather that our ML friends assured us was normal, a succession of cold, westerly gales. When the tide runs against the wind a short, steep sea builds up just the wrong distance between crests for small craft. In these conditions MLs and chasers alike were continuously swept and occasionally buried in foaming crests which came aboard knee deep. Life lines were a must.

One calm, sunny day we had just returned from patrol. A dispatch from the British requested that Unit 1 detach a subchaser to proceed to a position that was about ten miles from Weymouth to tow in a seaplane reported down. As *No. 143* had already fueled, George directed me to undertake the task and advised the British that *No. 143* would depart at once.

The plane was one of the Channel Air Patrol engaged in spotting enemy subs, a little unarmed, two-place fabric biplane on pontoons. They could take off and land only on a calm surface.

Channel weather and the prevalence of sudden fog made this type of antisubmarine patrol so hazardous that plane mortality was said to be 150 per cent a year, yet to the credit of the service there was no dearth of volunteer pilot replacements.

The surface was like a lake. We spotted the plane from five miles away and ranged within hailing distance. It appeared undamaged but there was no sign of life aboard. We put over the wherry and took the end of a towline to the plane. Chadwick made the line fast to a mooring fixture forward while I climbed into the pilot's cockpit. The gasoline gauge showed half full, there was no indication of fire, and nothing seemed disturbed. The observer's cockpit the same. The crew had vanished.

This mystifying situation we reported by radio phone. *No. 143* then proceeded toward Weymouth at eight knots with the plane in tow.

The sea remained calm, but thunderheads began to build up over the land, sure warning of one of the lashing rain squalls occasionally experienced at this season, much thunder and lightning with a blast of wind that soon subsided.

I made a major miscalculation. Being unfamiliar with airplanes I neglected to lash the control stick in its full forward position. When the squall, a particularly vicious one, struck I naturally headed *No. 143* into it. So, naturally, did the plane take off. It rose vertically the length of the tow line, which was about one hundred feet, then snubbed and crashed in a nose dive that narrowly missed our stern and the twelve depth charges in the racks. The plane hit the water hard enough to disintegrate. The engine sank. The wreckage we had to cut away.

On our return to port, the British took the loss of the plane without comment, being only concerned with the fate of the crew. I was courteously thanked for my efforts and not blamed for my mistake.

As far as I know there was no support for any theory as to what had happened. The two men were listed missing in action on the supposition that they had landed for some unexplained reason and then been taken prisoner by an enemy submarine.

On two occasions during our turn in port we were requested by the British to put to sea: once to try to locate an enemy sub believed to be on the bottom within a mile of the harbor, and once to patrol the route of a large convoy while passing the vicinity of a submarine suspected to be lying in wait for it for which no adequate escort was available.

One of my pleasantest recollections of Weymouth was an evening when George and I were invited aboard one of the MLs for drinks and music. The skipper was the composer of "The Song of the Sea Slugs," a dirge that we had not yet heard in its entirety.

Our host produced from a locker a box about the size of a cradle. When legs were unfolded it proved to be an eight octave piano with standard keys. Two stirrups hanging from beneath controlled the pedal action. He explained that its compactness was attained by the hammers striking tuning forks instead of strings, consequently it could never get out of tune. The hammers were of some synthetic material impervious to moisture; in fact this instrument was developed by a firm in Scotland for the missionary trade in jungle stations where no piano or organ could survive the climate. The pitch, of course, was absolutely true and the volume and resonance more than adequate for a tiny ML wardroom.

The skipper was a musician of no mean calibre, with a fine repertory of ribald British songs. He raised the subject of American jazz, which he confessed he had been unable to master. George asked if he might ask one of his engine-room crew aboard to demonstrate jazz as it was played in New Orleans. In all my experience I have never heard McAllister's equal in playing by ear. He started off with "Basin Street Blues." Not another soul could be jammed in that small wardroom; a score crowded on deck to listen. I dare say Mac was the first enlisted man to be inducted into a British wardroom except on duty or to be balled out, but these British officers, observing that in playtime we accepted Mac as an equal, took the same attitude and plied him too with drinks.

Eight officers of His Majesty's and Mr. Daniels' Navy harmonized their hearts out, followed by a late meal concocted aboard *No. 177.*

The Song of the "Sea Slugs"

Sing me a song of a frail M. L.,
    May the Lord have mercy upon us;
Rolling about in an oily swell,
    May the Lord have mercy upon us;
Out on a high explosive spree,
Petrol, lydite, and TNT,

Looking for U-boat 303,
  May the Lord have mercy upon us.

Sing me a song of a bold young "lieut."
  May the Lord have mercy upon us;
Two gold bands on an "owed for suit,"
  May the Lord have mercy upon us;
Ship the cable and full ahead,
Hard a starboard and heave the lead,
The detonators are in my bed,
  May the Lord have mercy upon us.

Sing me a song of a bright young "sub."
  May the Lord have mercy upon us;
A terribly ignorant, half-baked cub,
  May the Lord have mercy upon us;
Of the king's regulations he knows not one,
He has left undone what he ought to have done,
And Oh! My Lord, when he fires that gun,
  May the Lord have mercy upon us.

Sing me a song of a CMB [engineer],
  May the Lord have mercy upon us;
Bred in a garage and sent to sea,
  May the Lord have mercy upon us;
Taken away from the motor trade,
Seasick, sorry, and sore dismayed,
But a hell of a "Knut" on the Grand Parade,
  May the Lord have mercy upon us.

Sing me a song of the ML cook,
  May the Lord have mercy upon us;
With a petrol stove in a greasy nook,
  May the Lord have mercy upon us;
Our meals a lukewarm lingering death,
We'll praise the Hun with our final breath
If he'll strafe our galley and slay our chef,
  May the Lord have mercy upon us.

Sing me a song of a North Sea base,
  May the Lord have mercy upon us;
A dirty forgotten one-horse place,

May the Lord have mercy upon us;
When the wind blows west how brave we are!
When the wind blows east it's different far,
We wish we were back in the Harbour Bar,
May the Lord have mercy upon us.

On June 15 a dispatch from *Aylwin* directed Unit 2 to join Unit 1 at Weymouth. When accounts were settled ashore the two units were to proceed in company to Plymouth, there to report for duty to Commander United States Naval Base 27. Our pay accounts were delivered to the base by *Aylwin*.

With regret George and I gave up our lodgings. While awaiting the arrival of Unit 2 from patrol, all accounts in the town were settled. A round of farewell calls on our British friends were pleasantly bibulous. The United States Navy must have made a good impression in Weymouth. For our part we departed with respect and admiration for the Royal Navy Volunteer Reserves serving in the sea slugs.

Chapter 9

Subchaser Base 27—Plymouth—Patrols—Armistice

JUNE 16 on a clear cold afternoon, Units 1 and 2 entered Plymouth harbor in column, one boat's length between chasers. Base 27 was easily identifiable by a forest of masts and antennae in a slip between two piers of jetty stone at the head of the harbor. It was overlooked by a high half-mile-long promenade called The Hoe, which was fronted by several hotels and flanked at one end by the red and white column of the old Eddystone light. This famous lighthouse had been removed stone by stone to be relocated ashore when a new one replaced it on the dangerous Eddystone Rocks ten miles south of Plymouth. It was on The Hoe that Sir Francis Drake was engaged in a game of bowls when the Spanish Armada was sighted.

The pier that we approached was the one from which the *Mayflower* sailed on its historic voyage. Using cavalry arm signals passed from bridge to bridge, our six chasers stopped engines simultaneously. The slip appeared to be filled with chasers. Moored two abreast on one side and three abreast on the other, a space was left just wide enough for our column to coast silently to the head of the slip where we spied an empty area. How were we to know that it was reserved as a turning basin for the admiral's barge, then absent! While crews on either side of the slot through which we were slowly moving rushed for fenders we berthed neatly across the head of the slip, three on one side, two on the other, the sixth chaser filling the gap. The maneuver was accomplished under the apprehensive eyes of all the gold braid on the base gathered to witness our arrival.

Subsequently we learned that these gentlemen had never seen chasers handled accurately and did not know it could be done. None of the new chasers we were joining had had enough opportunity or experience in coping with air-starting-and-reversing gas engines.

Our ships may have been lacking in paint and the crew short of uniforms, but they were efficient. Everything was clean, guns lubricated, all deck gear properly stowed and secured for sea. By comparison the new chasers in their fresh, shiny paint were a mess on deck. When we got acquainted with the new outfits they seemed to us as callow as a freshman home for his first vacation. They pooh-poohed the idea that hunting, or rather finding enemy submarines required experience or skill. Having as yet had no patrol experience they really believed that the waters teemed with submarines and attacks a daily occurrence.

Some sort of reputation preceded us to the base, probably due to that dispatch from Admiral Sims quoting the British approval of our performance, plus our familiarity with British signals and code systems. At any rate, Units 1 and 2 were accorded a sort of glamor not really merited.

All the administrative officers on the base were keyed up to feel that the chasers must be continuously at hair trigger pitch. They didn't stop to think that Units 1 and 2 could be just a bit fed up on the work and had been through experiences the newcomers knew nothing about.

We were scheduled during our in-port periods to sit through long study periods and lectures at headquarters on stuff that we knew from trial would not work, owing to lack of visibility, sea conditions, or sound interference. Of course it would be the essence of bad form, having been attached to the base so short a time, to imply we knew anything, so we kept our mouths shut.

The operations officer who controlled our destinies was the famous naval aviator, Commander T. G. "Spuds" Ellyson, USN, the first man in the Navy to take off a plane from the deck of a ship.

Regular patrol schedules when we arrived had not yet been established. George and I were given temporary assignments as instructors, taking successive groups of officers out in the harbor to practice by coming alongside each other.

We settled down to a new life, pay accounts taken up, with the added luxuries of a commissary and a ship's service department. Units 1 and 2 were given time to paint ship and restore equipment before starting regular patrols of four days on and four days off, the in-port period largely devoted to instruction sessions and endless inspections.

The fleet had a number of assorted pets, dogs, cats, and one monkey. Although it was no life for an animal I had an uncontrollable urge to acquire a dog of my own; Sally and I had always loved dogs, they were a part of our lives, and somehow I felt, however unreasonably, that having a dog would bring her closer.

An ad in the Plymouth newspaper offered pedigreed English bulldog puppies. The advertiser proved to be a Mrs. Gerald Cox, wife of the colonel commanding the garrison in Plymouth who bred bulldogs. I inspected her kennels and fell in love with a white male puppy with brown markings who seemed to want to adopt me, a very endearing trait. His name was Barrabas, and he was ten months old. He was aptly named, for he proved to be a thief—anything from my slippers to an unguarded dish. I probably paid too much for him because of a pedigree which was real and dated way back, but there must have been a bar sinister in his family because his points, which were otherwise perfect, were ruined by a tail which no bulldog aspiring to lineage should wear. It was full two inches too long and instead of the quirk it should have was straight as a pencil. From the beginning we understood each other perfectly.

Barry made no little contribution to the morale of the crew who took a proprietary interest in his welfare. He was equipped with a harness instead of a collar. On deck a light chain connected him to a wire strung from the back of the pilot house to the antenna mast aft so that he had the run of the deck. He was usually on deck except when I was off watch. Then he shared my bunk, wedged between me and the side of the ship. Like all his breed he snored, but I was usually too tired to disturb him.

One sunny morning four weatherstained, filthy mail sacks were delivered aboard *No. 143*, the long awaited mail from home via Bermuda and Corfu. The last mail we had received was in Bermuda in early March, four long months ago. As there was no wind the crew gathered on the forward deck where one sack at a time was dumped at their feet. To avoid scrambling, two men were assigned to pick up each piece of mail and read off the name of the addressee.

When the second sack was dumped, all hands recoiled. A doting mother in the midwest had mailed to her darling a couple of roast chickens. The mail from that sack was laid aside in fresh air for later attention. In spite of the chicken, it was a gala day for all hands.

I had a windfall of love letters from Sally, together with several small packages proving her clairvoyance in what I most needed.

The six skippers in Division 4 came to have both respect and affection for Commander Ellyson. We knew his career in naval aviation had been adventurous and distinguished. His desk job as operations officer and nursemaid to a group of naval neophytes he suffered with philosophical grace. Off duty he was good company and not averse to joining junior reserve officers in the bar parlor at the Globe.

The day before Unit 1 was to embark on its first patrol, he briefed us, together with the three skippers in Unit 2 which would relieve us.

We gathered around the board in Operations on which was a master chart covering the area in which we were to operate. Units 1 and 2 were now designated as Division 4 of Squadron 2. The commander used a pointer.

"Because Division 4 is by far the most experienced now operating, you boys get the toughest assignment. From Longships lightship off Land's End to the Scilly Islands, here, the distance is fifteen miles. Six miles off Land's End is Seven Stones lightship. The nine miles between it and the nearest of the islands is not navigable, a mess of rocks. Over here, about ten miles east of Seven Stones is Wolf Rock lighthouse. Your patrol area is the triangle formed by these three marks. To make it more difficult, the lightships and Wolf Rock are blacked out for the duration. No sound signals.

"The enemy has not mined the passage between Land's End and Seven Stones so he can move submerged between the English Channel and the Irish Sea. The Allies need to use it, so it has not been mined by our side, either.

"Tides from the Channel and the Irish Sea meet in this area. A westerly gale setting against a four-knot ebb current causes such a sea that even big ships elect to pass outside the Scillys. The rise and fall of tide averages twenty-three feet.

"It is obvious that subchasers can't maintain station in such conditions. We don't expect them to. The problem that you will

Berth at Plymouth

"Subchaser cit," Plymouth, 1918

face is to judge the weather to determine when to run for shelter, where to go, and how much time to allow in order to make it.

"It is the presence of the subchasers in considerable numbers that will keep enemy submarines down rather than their capacity to attack them. Even if you never get a chance to attack, we want you to stay out there as long as you can without risking the loss of a chaser, which would be as costly to the cause as if sunk by the enemy.

"Don't forget that most aids to navigation, such as buoys and range marks have been removed. The only lighthouse lit on the whole south coast of England is Eddystone. The south coast of Cornwall is high and bold. I am told the native fishermen standing in for the coast determine their distance off by blowing the whistle and timing the echo. Soundings don't help much because the water is deep and the bottom uniformly level right up to the land except for offshore ledges.

"Now let's consider possible ports of refuge from your patrol area. St. Catherine's harbor in the Scilly Isles is the nearest, but you had better forget it. The approach is only from the west where your gales come from, and the unmarked channel is too narrow and twisting to attempt, even though once around the point of the harbor you would have a safe anchorage.

"The two nearest fishing ports in Cornwall are St. Ives on the north coast and Penzance in Mount's Bay on the south coast. Each has a walled basin with a cobblestoned bottom, called 'the hard,' which dries out at low tide. Fishermen come in with the tide and ground out against the seawall, carrying lines ashore from their masts to prevent falling over. In neither of these ports would there be room enough for three of you to tie up inside, and not enough shelter to anchor safely outside. Anyway, if you grounded out you would risk damaging your listening gear.

"Your logical refuge is Falmouth, safe in all weather, a big-ship harbor protected from submarine attack by a mine net. Contact mines are secured to the net from the bottom up to six feet below the surface. The net is suspended from a cable from shore to shore supported by drums. The single entrance is narrow, marked by two unlighted buoys. From your patrol area you would have to allow time for a run of about twenty miles from the nearest point of your patrol area to this entrance. In a rising westerly gale you would be in a lee of sorts once you had rounded the Lizard. This is a high, steep promontory. I am told there is a dangerous tide rip, some acres in area, south of the point and that the distance off is unpredictable, varying from one to five miles depending on combinations of wind and tide direction.

"Well, there it is, gentlemen. You have the picture as far as I can give it to you. Follow established hunting procedures as weather permits. Unit 1 will be relieved by Unit 2 in the usual manner and will then return to Plymouth, or if in a port of refuge, so report."

Ellyson was a refreshing contrast to some of the officers attached to the base, which was developing into a stiff-necked Navy regulations affair like New London à la Spafford. The reserves had volunteered their services for a wartime contribution, not adopted the Navy as a life's profession. Often the attitude of the regular Navy officers was that nothing more desirable could be conceived than the life of an officer, USN. These few literally could not understand the reserves' desire to get home, their service over with, the sooner the better.

That first patrol was uneventful. Moderate seas and good visibility enabled us to familiarize ourselves visually with the boundaries of our patrol area and the topography of the land. This proved fortunate indeed. A good deal of shipping afforded practice in listening procedures but no enemy contacts were made. Duly relieved, we returned to base, arriving early morning of the fifth day out.

On its second patrol Unit I encountered dense fog in the triangle off Land's End. After two days and two nights of being carried hither and yon by the tides in our normal stop-listen-start patrol procedure, when it came time to depart for Plymouth we had no point of departure from which to lay a course. We discussed over the phone the wisdom of steaming north until we made a landfall, then following the coast until we could identify something recognizable. We decided the coast of Cornwall in the Land's End area in the existing absence of visibility was too dangerous to approach on account of innumerable outlying ledges and no aids to navigation. The unit that had relieved us by telephone was out of sound range and might be anywhere in the patrol area. There was not a breath of wind. That we were in a strong tide was evidenced by dimples on the surface. We were out of sight of each other. George said he had a hunch we were in the vicinity of Wolf Rock and if we steered west magnetic for twenty miles we would either find the tide rip off the Lizard or get an echo off high land. Jack Morse in *No. 148* and I said we were lost and knew it.

I stepped out on the bridge for another look at the impenetrable smother when I heard a sound fairly close abeam, the sound of water lapping on a shore. I literally felt my scalp prickle. The men heard it, too.

"Stand by port and starboard engines," I yelled, "Up tube!"

Suddenly, dead ahead, where there had been nothing, was a great round rock as high as the pilot house not three chaser lengths distant, toward which we were being set broadside by the tide. It was well that we had identified visually the boundaries of our assigned triangle for I recognized it at once as South Stone, the largest of the rocky islets between Seven Stones lightship and the Scilly Isles, some six miles northwest of Martin's Island. The chart showed deep water to the northwest where we were, so I maneuvered to keep in sight of South Stone while *No.'s 177* and *148* got bearings on my propeller sounds to enable them to come within sight.

They agreed that this was indeed South Stone and that we now had a definite point of departure for the run to clear the Lizard.

I said to George, "If we'd played your hunch to steer west magnetic, assuming we were at Wolf Rock, in seventeen miles we would have piled up on The Brissons this side of Cape Cornwall — and that's the worst graveyard of offshore ledges on the Cornish coast."

He laughed. "It was just dumb luck you stumbled on South Stone, and you know it. Well, let's put the show on the road. Home, James, and don't spare the horses. Course one two zero magnetic, distance thirty-five miles to abeam of the Lizard. Speed ten, echelon formation, visual contact."

I said to Connolly, "The moral of this little scare is, 'always case the joint first and remember what you see'."

"I'll do just that," he replied soberly.

In Plymouth George, Jack Morse, and I usually went ashore together, starting our evening at the bar parlor of the Globe. Not as yet having made local acquaintanceships, we found the fleshpots of Plymouth unenticing. Seventy-five per cent of the town's population seemed to be women, many with bad teeth, mostly in uniform, Wrens, British and American nurses, messengers, taxi chauffeurs, and truck drivers. The men, except for a few of the very old, were one and all in uniform, on leave or invalided home.

The next patrol was to say the least different.

There were no enemy contacts, but the second day on station the weather worsened, giving barometric evidence of the makings of a westerly gale. We discussed the portents. George elected to run for shelter at Falmouth. Had we had more experience we would have started sooner. By the time we were abeam of the Lizard it was dark. Tide ebbing against the gale had built up a steep, breaking sea from astern, just the wrong length for a chaser. George wisely ordered speed reduced to midship engine only in order to keep a propeller buried. The two wing propellers were rolled to the surface. The motion was wild. I could see only intermittently the blue light on *No. 177* from where I stood on the bridge, hanging on to a machine gun and spitting salt water. At times we were swept from astern by five feet of solid green water. Two men at the wheel worked hard to keep the ship from broaching.

With appalling suddenness, out of the night almost above my head on the starboard beam lifted the rearing, shadowy bulk of the head sails and bows of a big sailing vessel. It was too late to stop. To the man watching me from the pilot-house window I made the emergency gesture we had arranged for full speed ahead, all engines. Fortunately the wing engines were still warm. The response was instant and we made it in two plunges — a regular submarine crash dive. The vessel's bow came down so close across our stern, just missing the depth charges, that tons of water from her bow wave fell on our decks as we scuttled out from under, clearing her by but literally a few feet. As she disappeared, swallowed up in the night to a chorus of startled yells, we narrowly missed ramming the stern of *No. 177.* George squawked indignantly in the telephone. He had not even glimpsed the vessel that had so nearly sunk us.

For weeks I had nightmares about the narrowness of our escape.

Past an invisible Lizard we changed course for Falmouth and found outselves in the lee of the promontory. The gale was as strong but the sea smoothed out. George decided we could never find the entrance buoys until daylight, so decided to work up close to shore west of the net and there anchor in a small bight shown on the chart as Swanpool Beach. Here we were well protected from any sea except a chop, but the wind came down off the high land in fierce gusts. The three chasers anchored a hundred yards apart in ten fathoms. *No. 143* put out the heavy anchor on 300 feet of chain. Although we yawed considerably the anchor appeared to be holding. An anchor watch of two men was set, one on deck and one manning the phone in the pilot house. Before turning in I used a yachting precaution of putting overboard the sounding lead, which weighed about ten pounds. With enough slack in the line to allow for the yawing, I carried the end below and secured it to my wrist. If *No. 143* dragged anchor unperceived by the watch, the line tugging at my wrist would wake me.

So it did. At the first crack of dawn a tug on the line roused me, at once aware that the motion had changed; we were more nearly broadside to the chop and no longer yawing. In two minutes I was in the pilot house calling down the voice tube to the engineer on duty to stand by for signals. He replied that we had no air and would be unable to start for about fifteen minutes.

I looked over the side in the direction of our drift. We were undeniably slowly dragging anchor, and to my horror I made out in the half-light a line of oil drums toward which we were gradually drifting. The Falmouth mine net was close under our lee.

Grabbing the phone, I roused George. "Okay," he said crisply when I had described the situation, "I'll be over just as soon as I buoy my anchor. Rig towing hawsers forward and aft on your windward side with a heaving line rigged to each. Bring the heaving lines amidships. I'm coming in bow on to your broadside. Pass the two heaving lines across to my bow. We'll secure the two hawsers to my forward bitts and back away, dragging you off broadside. By that time you may be down on the nets. As I pull you off you take up your anchor. When we are well clear of the net I'll slip the stern hawser and tow you bow to bow until you are where you can anchor again. Understood?"

I gave him an affirmative. When he pulled us off, exactly as directed, we were almost on the net. If he had not known just what to do and how to do it, *No. 143* and probably *No. 177* would have been blown up with all hands. We actually saw the top mines. The entire ship's company of *No. 143* was still shaken when an hour later we were safely moored in Falmouth harbor.

The eager beaver on duty in the engine room, believing *No. 143* safely at anchor for the rest of the night, had goofed. Without asking permission he had released the air supply to dismantle an air line that had developed a slow leak. He will never do that again! The enormity of what might have happened was punishment enough.

The next patrol was calm with dense fog. Off Wolf Rock we made a definite contact on a submarine that had submerged when it heard our propellers. We tracked the wily beast for three hours without being able to close for an attack, then lost him in sound interference from a British armed trawler named *Wild Rose* out of Falmouth, which came close enough to inquire if we had made any enemy contact. She asked us to keep a lookout for bodies from a torpedoed British hospital ship, *Llandovery Castle.*

When we returned to Plymouth we were told that German submarines, after torpedoing a ship, often lurked in the vicinity to get a shot at any vessel answering an SOS from the victim. Accordingly a policy was adopted that ordered vessels drawing more than six feet to stay out of the area. Units 3 and 4 of Division 5, in whose area the hospital ship had been sunk, later found a number of bodies floating in life jackets, their faces eaten by fish. They brought in the ID tags. From these chaser crews we learned that the bodies of men float face down, women always face up. Many of the *Llandovery Castle* bodies were nurses.

Ensign Ashley D. Adams was the skipper of *No. 137* in Division 6. I had met him once in college days when he rowed seven on the Yale freshman crew and I rowed seven on the Harvard crew. Our renewed acquaintance brought us in close association. One day, when by chance, we were in Operations, Commander Ellyson was talking on the telephone. He beckoned to us. We heard him say, "Very well, a car will pick you up at the Dockyard in Devenport at 1400. Hope you have a good game."

He chuckled. "Here is a job for you two. Lieutenant Commander Brown and Lieutenant Commander LeBreton command destroyers, which at the moment are berthed at the Dockyard, Devenport, across the harbor. They have asked me to provide two junior officers and transportation to wherever they can get a game of golf. I am told there is a golf course of sorts at Yelverton about five miles out of town northeast of the city. It is up on the edge of the moors."

Ashley spoke up. "I've been there, sir. Not much of a course, but a wonderful old pub. This being Saturday I imagine it will be crowded with the farmers for miles around having their Saturday night binge."

"I'll give you a chit to the supply officer to let you take one of the base cars. Take your clubs along and be at Devenport in plenty of time."

We returned to our ships to spruce up for the expedition. I told Ashley I knew Commander LeBreton, but did not tell him I did not play golf. Having no civilian sports clothes, we reported in uniform.

The car provided, like all base personnel vehicles, was a Model T Ford touring car, complete with top and side curtains, a spare tire, and a full tank of petrol. Complying with rules established by DORA (Defense of the Realm Act) the headlight glass was painted dark blue, leaving only a pinpoint of light in the center, hardly conducive to night driving.

We embarked the two officers and their golf bags and in holiday spirits proceeded to the Yelverton public house, which doubled as club house for the golf facilities. It was shortly before the hour the bar could legally open for business. By this time fog and drizzle in which we had started became a steady downpour. At a long railing outside the building were tethered some twenty dejected looking moor ponies patiently awaiting their masters' return. Each carried a sack of hay as a saddle.

Inside a low ceilinged room a bedlam of voices and laughter met us. Wall lamps cast a cozy glow through a haze of smoke redolent of tobacco and wet wool. Farmers lined up at the long bar paid no heed to our entrance. The proprieter, flanked behind the bar by two laughing barmaids, had his eye on the clock.

Finally he shouted, "Gentlemen!"

Dextrously the mugs of 'alf and 'alf were filled and slid across the counter by six busy hands. When earlier comers had been served the United States Navy was able to obtain four warm pink gins. "This will do for a starter. Cheers!" said Captain LeBreton. "As golf seems to be cancelled by weather, I propose to establish an entente cordiale with the local farm community."

He made an impassioned patriotic speech, ending in toasts to the king and to the president of the United States. The two lieutenant commanders paid for several rounds of drinks. Presently, at the suggestion of the proprietor we Americans moved to the bar parlor where we were served beefsteak and kidney pie.

Promptly at nine o'clock, preceded by a last call for drinks, the proprietor closed the bar. Nobody felt any pain. The bar population straggled out to the drenched ponies among a chorus of goodnights. After seeing the ponies disappear in all directions we returned to the barroom to find a solitary farmer asleep in a chair oblivious of the departure of his fellows. We roused him with difficulty, intending to help him board his pony. When we got him outside, there was no pony left at the rail. Someone in untying his own pony must have released the missing animal, which had probably wisely decided to go home.

Captain LeBreton as senior officer present assumed command of the situation. He announced that the United States Navy would never forsake an ally; we would load the farmer aboard the Ford and deliver him to his home as directed by him. With some difficulty placed in the back seat between LeBreton and Brown, he again went sound asleep. The side curtains were buttoned down and the upper half of the windshield folded. I drove, with Ashley keeping a watchful eye on his edge of the road. The pinpoint of light from the headlights revealed the road only a few car lengths ahead.

I had no idea where we were going. We started along a road heading toward the moor. LeBreton poked the farmer awake and asked him if we were on the right road. The farmer's grunt was interpreted as an affirmative. At a fork we stopped for further interpretation of the farmer's unintelligible responses. LeBreton claimed he understood the man perfectly and directed me to take the left fork. On account of rain and fog visibility was now almost nil. We still proceeded in low gear. Ten minutes later, after passing a couple of intersections, a narrow track between hedgerows led off to the right. We stopped while LeBreton again roused the farmer to ask if this was his place. He struggled to get out.

Brown said, "I guess this is it. He wants to get out."

"Perhaps he just wants to be sick," said Ashley. "Maybe we ought to find out."

"Turn down here. It's probably the road to his farm."

The space between the hedgerows was little wider than the car. We proceeded gingerly down an increasingly steep grade. I stood on the brake. As we slid down into an open area an unseen mound of gravel on the left gently capsized the car against the bank on the right at an angle of $45°$.

"Now hear this!" LeBreton roared. "All hands abandon ship!"

With some difficulty the curtains on the upper side were

unbuttoned and the doors opened. We had entered the floor of a large gravel pit. The farmer was carried tenderly to a bed of gravel some distance from the car where he was sick. Again he passed out.

"I guess this wasn't his farm," said Brown. "You misread the signals, David."

"Let's put Lizzie on her feet and get her turned around. Then we've got to get her up that grade. Let's go."

With spinning wheels, the three men pushing, she was nursed out of the pit. Back on the road, they piled in.

"Where to, Captain?" I said. The rain was moderating, but the fog grew denser by the minute.

"Think we can reverse course to Yelverton?"

"No, sir, but we can proceed in that direction. Might take us off the moor. The base ought to equip their cars with compasses. We took so many turns and forks I've lost track of north."

"Carry on a while. See if we recognize any roads. No road signs allowed in England during wartime, you know."

So eventually we pulled up beside the road to doze fitfully until dawn light showed us which direction was east. Damp, cold and hungry we reached Devenport at 0800.

"Do you know," said Captain LeBreton as we sat down to breakfast in *Aylwin*'s wardroom after hot showers, "we forgot all about that damned farmer. Wonder if he found his way home after he slept it off."

"More probably some centuries from now his bones will be found and identified as a Piltdown man," said Brown.

"He won't know the difference," I said. "Just remember he died happy."

A unit from Division 6 relieved Unit 2 for our next scheduled patrol period. We were sent on a special mission to an area a hundred miles west of Brest. Fast transports that had delivered troops in Brest returned unescorted across the area homeward bound. Except in the English Channel troopships were not provided with escorts if they were capable of twenty-five knots or better. In this area a number of enemy attacks on fast transports had been attempted without success. Our job was to try to spot submarines known to be lurking in the area and send position reports and warnings to all shipping in the vicinity.

The weather was kind. When we reported on station we were advised that USS *Mount Vernon* (formerly *Kronprinzessin Cecilie*) was due to pass through our area at 1200 hours, making zigzag courses at twenty-seven knots. At 1100 the crows-nest lookouts on all three chasers reported a surfaced submarine on the horizon—quite possibly Penmarche Pete. Warning was promptly sent. The sub submerged almost at once, long before we were close enough for a sound contact. We approached the estimated position and made a good contact just as the *Mount Vernon* appeared over the horizon. This contact we reported to her. Unfortunately it was soon drowned out by the noise of her big propellers.

The submarine made a lucky guess as to the ship's next change of course. We watched helplessly while a torpedo found its target, a hit beneath the bridge. The portion of the hole that showed above the waterline was big enough to drive a truck through. The *Mount Vernon* headed back for Brest, her speed only reduced by a few knots. We figured we could be more useful trying to regain contact than by attempting to follow a ship that we could not hope to overtake.

I learned after the war from an officer who had been on the bridge of *Mount Vernon* at the time, the torpedo had struck in unoccupied troop quarters. The watertight doors were closed. Miraculously nobody was killed or even injured.

We were unable to make further contact. When little more than enough fuel remained to reach Plymouth, we started home, a run of thirty-six hours, mostly in fog.

The going was uncomfortable, the ship rolling through an arc of 20°. Dancy came up to the pilot house accompanied by Scheuerman, one of the machinist's mates, who was a self-appointed pharmacist's mate with ambitions to study for a medical career. It was he who treated minor injuries such as burns, cuts, and abrasions.

Dancy said, "Scheuerman wants you to look at the cook's arm, captain. Loden fell against one of his cooking knives a couple of days ago and got quite a nasty gash. Scheuerman cleaned the wound as best he could, drew it together, and bandaged it tight. He thinks the wound has become infected and wants you to tell him what to do."

I looked inquiringly at Scheuerman, a husky, clean-cut youth of twenty, one of our most responsible crew members. He looked serious and worried.

"You can see a bright red discoloration that has been moving up his arm in the last few hours. It looks like blood poisoning to me. The book says that kind of an infection moves pretty fast. I think he ought to be in a hospital and have it cleaned out. If it continues unchecked he might lose his arm. How long before we make port, sir?"

"Something like thirty-six hours if we're not delayed by weather."

Scheuerman shook his head. "He will be a pretty sick man by that time if that arm isn't operated on. At least that is my guess."

"I'll have a look at it. Loden never complains, so this infection must have got too much of a start."

We found Loden, obviously in pain, trying to start the noon meal.

I said to Dancy, "Break out Webb and Cayron. Tell them they are to take over the cook's duties until further orders." To Loden I said, "Come on now, George, you're in no shape to cook. As of now you are relieved of all duty. Lie down on the bunk there and let me look at that arm."

Scheuerman removed the bandage. The cut was on the underside of the forearm half-way between wrist and elbow, a gash about three inches long. A bright red line had moved above the similar discoloration around the incision. "See what I mean, sir? That line has moved an inch in the last hour."

I was faced with a major decision. That arm required immediate surgery, as was only too obvious. I could not order Scheuerman to do the job, or anyone else. It was up to me alone.

I said to Scheuerman, "I'm going to open the arm and I need your help. We have an adequate medical kit. It has the equipment we need. Fetch it here and I will pick out what has to be sterilized. I'll want plenty of boiling water and a bucket of hot water for hand wash. When we are all ready we'll lash him to the mess table and lash the arm so he can't move it. In the meantime I want to refresh my memory from the drawings in that medical textbook. It is several years since I handled a scalpel in a course in physiology in college to dissect dead cats. The book I want to have open at the right place is in the medical kit. Get moving."

I knew what I had to do, apply a tourniquet to the brachial artery, make enough of an incision to clean out all the affected tissue, fill the area with sulphur powder, put in a drainage wick in two parts so that it could be removed from both ends, and sew up the wound over the wicks.

While Scheuerman was on his errand I went on deck for a look at the weather and to brief Connolly on what we were doing. I told him to report to *No. 177*. The fog held; there was still a heavy swell but not much wind.

When Scheuerman returned, while we were still out of earshot of the patient, he asked the question that was uppermost in my mind.

"What are you going to use for anaesthetic, sir? There is nothing in the medical supplies."

"The Navy sure slipped up when they issued a complete surgical kit and no anaesthetic. I am just going to have to try psychology and hope to God it works."

"What do you mean, sir?"

"I'm going to try to scare him into fainting. If it works he'll be unconscious for a little while at least. After we lash him to the table I want to be lashed to the stanchion at the aft end of the table so I won't have to be balancing while I'm working."

Scheuerman replied, "Guess you have everything planned, sir. After the stuff is sterilized I'll lay it out. You call for what you want."

"Don't you faint on me, too. I need you."

"I won't, sir."

Fortunately I had watched one or two operations and had an idea of what I would need to have sterile, including threaded curved needles, forceps, scissors, and gauze sponges. Also I refreshed my memory of how to tie a surgeon's knot, so that I could tie off the stitches as necessary.

The sleeping quarters of the black gang next to the galley provided a confined operating theatre, but handy to everything needed. The audience was attentive and cooperative. When the stage was set, surgeon and patient lashed firmly in place beneath a naked electric bulb, I waved the scalpel under George's nose and told him how much it was going to hurt. As hoped, he went out like a light. Unfortunately, as did two of the audience.

The tourniquet controlled the bleeding. Everything went as planned. After the wound was sewed up with twelve stitches I bandaged it tightly before releasing the tourniquet. He regained consciousness while I was sewing him up, but seemed to be in a state of shock. He did not suffer much at the time but had a miserable trip back to Plymouth where he was delivered to the base hospital. The only painkiller aboard was aspirin.

Loden missed the next patrol. He was returned fully recovered but with a nasty scar. The medical officer seemed to think I had done an adequate job. I decided that I would bootleg aboard a can of sulphuric ether in case there was a next time.

Scheuerman was a man of many parts. He loved to make doughnuts. When the ship was in port so that he could keep a kettle of hot fat on the stove without spilling he would produce a few batches, choosing a time between preparation of meals when stove space was available. He figured on two doughnuts for each member of the crew. He also had to pick a time when it was not raining so that the hatch above the stove could be wide open to let the smoke escape.

Since the incipient riot over the oil on the deck due to the use of the wrong hose by the black gang, there had been little or no friction between members of the crew. This happened on the passage between Bermuda and the Azores. Now again Connolly had to intervene in the matter of the doughnuts. Several members of the crew discovered that a bent wire on the end of a string could be used to hook a cooked doughnut out of the hot fat while Scheuerman had his back turned shaping more of them. The game was to hook a doughnut without being identified. Scheuerman's exasperation hit the flashpoint when he briefly recognized one face above the hatch. He swarmed up the ladder and caught the culprit in the act of eating a doughnut. One punch to the mouth smeared doughnut all over his face. Fortunately Mr. Connolly arrived in time to prevent further fisticuffs and personally to guard the rest of "Operation Doughnut." Scheuerman could not understand why all present, including Connolly, were convulsed with laughter. That batch of doughnuts was rationed.

Occasionally in our in-port periods there were unexpected invitations ashore. Sir Alec Winston and his lady occupied an ancestral castle outside Plymouth. Lady Mary called Operations to ask for two junior naval officers to round out a surprise dinner party she was giving to celebrate her husband's twenty-sixth birthday. She explained that she had eight young women and six British officers, but that men were in short supply. Perhaps two attractive Americans would solve this shortage and add a novel interest for the girls, all either young widows or wives whose husbands were at the front or at sea. Sir Alec, a captain of infantry, was home from the trenches on a four-day furlough.

Commander Ellyson tapped George Atwood and me, adding wistfully that he wished he were still a junior officer. If the other women were as charming as Lady Mary, whom he had met at a tea, we were in for a delightful evening. The base kindly furnished us a Model T.

A butler ushered us into a long, narrow, lofty room lit by candelabra high on the walls. A colorful party in full swing stood around a table laden with drinks presided over by our host. The women were young, wearing low necked, long evening gowns brilliant with jewelry. The men were young British in uniform, several wearing decorations. Lady Mary came forward to greet us. To the crowd who momentarily ceased their animated chatter and laughter, she announced, "Here are two American friends borrowed from the United States Navy, Lieutenant Atwood and Ensign Moffat. I shall not make formal introductions, they're so boring. I want each of you to introduce yourselves as opportunity offers. Carry on!"

The floor of the further half of the room was a step higher than where we were. Here a refectory table, lit by tall tapers, was set for eighteen, our host and hostess placed at the ends, eight chairs on either side. A white damask cloth reached nearly to the floor. Low bowls of flowers were spaced between the tapers. The floor of the entire room was strewn with rushes, the stone walls hung with tapestries and portraits. Under the watchful eye of the butler, three uniformed maids passed hors d'oeuvres and refilled glasses.

Both George and I were awed by the beauty of the scene but soon put at ease by a couple of vivacious, very lovely young women.

Sir Alec and his bride were evidently dog lovers. I counted six different breeds and sizes mingling with the guests, being fed tidbits. When we eventually sat down to dinner Sir Alec ordered them all under the table, where they obediently stayed. The butler maintained his post behind Sir Alec.

Presently Sir Alec whispered in the butler's ear. He was gone for ten minutes to reappear accompanied by a man wearing leggings and canvas jacket, the uniform of a gamekeeper, who carried a squirming sack. The maids and the butler withdrew, we assumed because we were at the moment between courses.

Sir Alec beckoned the grinning gamekeeper close. "Now!" he said. The sack was emptied under the table and pandemonium broke loose. The noise of a fight between two dogs is noisy enough, but when six dogs simultaneously attack an enemy that seems able to take care of itself, the noise is deafening. Everyone except Sir Alec and Lady Mary hastily pushed back their chairs. Our host and hostess moved only to raise a glass to each other, smiling. The ladies screamed and with one accord climbed on their chairs and raised their dresses high above their knees.

"Good show," said Sir Alec, when the screams had subsided. "This was planned by my wife, you know. She thought a touch of excitement would help the party. Gentlemen, I'll wager you have never before seen such an exquisite lot of legs in such effective display." The men roared their approval, raising wine glasses to Lady Mary who, still unmoving, laughed mischievously at the tableau she had created.

"I am sure the girls enjoyed the opportunity," she said demurely. "You may take the stoat away now, Giles."

Giles donned a pair of heavy gauntlets and dove into the melee under the table. He emerged dragging by the hind legs a nasty looking furry beast resembling a rat the size of a terrier. With some difficulty the stoat was stuffed in the sack.

"Any damage to the dogs?"

"Not that I can see, m'lord. They are licking a few cuts. If you ask me, sir, they enjoyed the party." He departed with his cargo.

A week later we learned that Sir Alec had died in France, a saddening note to add to the memory of a heartwarming party.

The ingenuity of young Americans in inventing amusements to occupy idle hours always surprised me. On which chaser the idea originated is unknown, but cockroach racing developed into a well-organized parimutuel system in which considerable pay changed hands. The cockroach population was not the problem on *No. 143* that it was on many of the less clean ships, but where there was food there were undeniably cockroaches living in the dark corners of lockers. Many of the skippers paid rewards in terms of hours of liberty upon presentation of dead cockroaches strung on a thread for counting. This led to the preservation of the larger cockroaches for the ship's racing stable. A white racing number was painted with a tiny brush on the roach's back. He was carefully kept in a box and fed for strength, then starved before a race for incentive to reach the food at the finish line.

Races were held after work hours on dry days on the forward deck of one of the chasers. Strips of wood two inches square were tacked to the deck two inches apart with a starting gate at one end of each course and a finish line at the other where was placed a morsel of the entrant's favorite food (preferably smelly).

Each roach had a handler equipped with a single twelve-inch straw from a broom. This he was allowed to use to urge the roach along the course under the watchful eye of the referee, who disqualified an entrant if the handler pushed it or shortened his hold on the straw.

Betting stations were established where one shilling and five shilling tickets were sold. On race day the enthusiasm was vociferous. Usually as many as a hundred men occupied every vantage point from which the course could be observed. Every roach had a name as well as a number by which it was exhorted.

Thus passed many exciting hours that might better have been used for self-improvement or writing home.

One recollection comes to mind: the picture of two grown men on their bellies on the galley floor intently watching a crack believed to be the domicile of an especially large and nimble cockroach that had so far evaded capture. This was a serious money-making occupation! If they could capture a winner they could sell it for as much as a pound sterling.

An American submarine reported to the base for temporary duty as a training target for the chaser fleet. Each unit went out in turn under the admiral's personal supervision. Mission: to locate the sub, then make a simulated attack. Very properly, he wanted to assess our hunting procedures and effectiveness.

Not until afterwards did we learn that the sub had eluded all the other units tested. Unit 1 was last to perform. By this time the admiral was unimpressed, not to say skeptical. Unit 1, through long experience, worked with a minimum of communications, the three boats as precisely simultaneous in every maneuver as though connected by wires.

We were told only the general area in which the sub would be found. The first hunt was a runaway. We sank our theoretical enemy with assurance and finesse. Then, to prove it was not accidental, we did it three times running on three different types of approach. On one attack *No. 143* was forced to go emergency full speed astern on three engines to avoid hitting the periscope that broke water a couple of hundred feet ahead.

The admiral's barge came alongside *No. 177* to hail by megaphone, "I didn't know how bad the others were until I saw your unit. Damn fine work. Well Done!" This from an officer who had never had a favorable word for anyone since he had taken command. We felt smug, even though we knew we were good.

Rumors at the base flew around like fuzz from dandelions. One that I hated to believe was that I was to be transferred from *No. 143* to command a division, the worst in the fleet, to bring it up to scratch. Happily for me the admiral's recommendation was lost in the shuffle. All transfers and promotions were henceforth to be handled in Washington by the Bureau of Navigation.

The promotion situation put the local command on the spot. In order to get best results from the chasers, temporary appointments were made regardless of rank. The executive officers in several chasers were now senior in rank to the ensigns commanding. Ashley Adams' unit and ours, still commanded by reserve officers, had the acknowledged reputation of being the most efficient in the fleet. George Atwood was still a lieutenant, junior grade, and Ashley, like me, was still an ensign, class 4, unqualified for sea duty. Our executive officers remained unchanged. The juggling of officers in the fleet was hardly conducive to morale.

An epidemic of what was called Spanish flu hit Plymouth. A ship that had sailed from Gibraltar with no illness on board reached Plymouth with two hundred dead, half the ship's company. It was not long before all hospital facilities in the city and at the base were taxed to capacity. Many of the chasers reported cases of high temperatures, which had to be treated aboard as there was no place to put them ashore.

Three men in my crew reported sick just as we were about to start on patrol. A British doctor helping out at the base told me that all the casualties from this epidemic appeared to be from the lungs suffusing from pneumonia. His directives were startling. When a man started to run a temperature he was to be lashed in his bunk in a sitting position and never allowed to be horizontal. To each

Subchaser No. 143

patient I was to administer two ounces of Scotch whiskey every hour until the fever broke. I reminded him that the United States Navy was dry and that the chasers were not even allowed to carry liquor as medical stores. He said that within the hour three cases of Scotch would be delivered to *No. 143* and not to ask any silly questions.

His prescription worked. There were no complaints about being lashed up in a sitting position. In fact, ours was a happy epidemic with no casualties.

Early in September we returned from a patrol that for me had no parallel. Everything conspired to make it rotten, mentally and physically. I had a touch of the Asian flu that was going the rounds, a cracking headache, and was continuously seasick for the two nights and one day I stayed on duty.

Off Wolf Rock in a westerly gale a sea broke over us and swept Barry overboard. We found his harness with a broken buckle hanging from his chain. We could not have maneuvered in that sea, even to pick up a man, let alone to find a little white dog. Nobody was to blame, but I couldn't help feeling guilty for having brought him aboard in the first place. It was no consolation that a college friend of mine, Shepley Nichols, was swept overboard from another chaser at about the same time. He was wearing a life jacket but was never recovered.

Connolly departed on a well-deserved four-day leave, his first since reporting for duty in Bermuda. He was headed for London with a gleam in his eye and a pocket full of accrued pay.

On his return, all smiles, he told me that he had met a charming Irish lady. He was never loquacious, but I gathered he had spent much of his leave in her apartment in bed. He said she was very hospitable.

He wrote her an effusive thank you letter, recalling some of their more tender moments. Then, possibly with a belated pang of conscience, he wrote his fiancée a stilted love letter as full of clichés as any letter I ever censored. He had told me in Bermuda that he was "sort of" engaged.

A month later, after receiving mail from home, he told me she had broken the engagement.

He said, "Mr. Moffat, I think women are unreasonable. She ought to know I wouldn't do a thing like that on purpose."

"A thing like what, for instance?"

"I got the letter to my London girl and to her in the wrong envelopes."

"Maybe they are unreasonable, at that," I said solemnly. He walked away shaking his head.

On the next patrol we witnessed an extraordinary accident at sea.

One of the fast Cunard liners, converted to a troop transport, was proceeding with an escort of four United States destroyers on a zigzag course headed up Channel. Unit 1 had been ordered to scout the area off Plymouth through which she was expected to pass.

The sea was calm, the visibility good. When the formation came in sight, one destroyer on each bow and one on each quarter, it was heading, at twenty-five knots, in the general direction of Plymouth by which I assumed that a change of course in their zigzag pattern was imminent. They passed a mile to the north of us then, sure enough, changed course 30° to the right, all except the destroyer on the starboard bow, which stayed on its original heading, obviously the victim of a steering malfunction.

A destroyer steaming at twenty-five knots cannot be brought to a stop suddenly, even with full reverse, nor can it be turned sharply with propellers going astern. A collision was unavoidable. It could not possibly cross the transport's bow. If it had maintained speed it would probably have been struck at the depth charges. If it went to full reverse, its sharp bow would have struck the transport amidships in the region of the boiler or engine rooms and done incalculable damage, if it did not sink her.

The destroyer's skipper stopped all engines with enough way on to allow his ship to be cut in two just forward of the bridge. He coolly calculated in the few seconds in which he had to reach a decision that the safety of the transport was his paramount responsibility. The bow of the transport would not be substantially damaged in cutting through the flimsy hull of a destroyer. The position of impact was gauged to a nicety. We heard the grinding crash a mile away. The destroyer's engine-room crew were still at station and the stern two-thirds of the ship promptly backed safely clear of the transport's side. Moments after the transport moved clear, the bow third sank in flames. The transport never paused.

When in the Channel we had noticed that the fast ships carried a power lifeboat swung out ready to lower. This transport was no exception. Even before the actual collision, the boat was manned and was in the process of being lowered, an indication of smart telephone work from the bridge. The moment the transport's keel passed above the destroyer's bridge the boat was lowered to the water, the automatic release gear activated just before it hit the surface. This type of gear is so designed that with a movement of one lever the stern is released a second before the bow. This prevents the boat from being tripped and swamped. If the sea was rough a launching under way could not, of course, be attempted. In this launching, the coxswain had the engine running before the boat was water borne. The whole episode was an impressive example of cool thinking and thorough training.

When Unit 1 arrived, men in life jackets who had been knocked overboard from the deck of the destroyer had already been picked up by the lifeboat and were being transferred to their ship.

George brought *No. 177* within hailing distance to ask how we could assist. The skipper asked us to stand by him until he reached Plymouth where he would proceed under his own power, stern first, steering with his propellers. He had asked for a tug to dock him on arrival at the Dockyard, Devenport. With the lifeboat in tow behind *No. 177*, we thus proceeded at eight knots to Plymouth fifteen miles distant. The destroyer moved its United States ensign to the bridge, which was now the stern.

We learned that eleven men had perished in the bow section, which sank too fast for their rescue or escape.

In Plymouth harbor, without further incident, the yard tug took over.

Rumors continued to fly, some of them pretty wild. The latest was that the first six chasers to reach Europe were to return to the United States to sell Liberty Bonds in the fourth loan campaign, than which nothing could be more unlikely. More specific was a letter from the Navy Department telling me that I had been admitted to the "competent class" of the reserve force without examination, from which I assumed that I was now in class 2 and eligible for sea duty and even ultimate promotion.

Another rumor, possibly not so wild, was that from each unit one officer and six enlisted men were to be selected to be sent back to the States in January to man the new 200-foot subchasers called Eagle boats under construction. The admiral, so went the rumor, would select the officer who in turn would select the six men.

Papers from home were the only information that reached us about Allied progress on the western front. The local press seemed to be thoroughly censored. We naturally distrusted published news of the alleged withdrawal of German submarines to their home ports, although recently no enemy contacts had been reported by the chaser fleet.

On November 11, news of the Armistice reached us at sea. Unit 1 was ordered to proceed from patrol area to a position twenty miles west of the Isle of Wight, there to await the arrival of a German submarine that would surrender to us by prearrangement. We were to escort it into Plymouth. If it had not appeared by 1600 hours we were to return to base.

The day was gray and rainy with an uncomfortable short chop. We arrived at the designated latitude and longitude at 1200 hours to spend in vain four hours of watchful waiting. The submarine failed to show. Every man aboard in his own way was charged with emotion, scarcely daring to believe that the war was actually at an end and home in sight. The younger ones whooped and sang and indulged in horseplay. My own solemn reaction was to bring my wife and children into sharp focus with the realization that for months I had been subconsciously thrusting them to the back of my mind, now at long last daring to be suffused by yearning. It was a glorious feeling for which I gave humble thanks to God.

On the way to Plymouth passing vessels dipped their colors, everyone waved and yelled like madmen. In the harbor all ships were dressed with flags. His Majesty's ships carried a bucket hoisted in the rigging, an international signal meaning "officers repair on board for drinks." One sailing vessel had an effigy of the kaiser hung at the yardarm, sword and all.

Ashore, simultaneously with the announcement of armistice, nationwide orders were posted closing all bars and restaurants. There was not much on hand available to drink, but a little went a long way. Pooled resources from several private diggings enabled us to throw quite a party, at which Commander Ellyson was a welcome guest.

The Defense of the Realm Act had not yet been rescinded, accordingly the city was still blacked out. The apartment in which we were foregathered was located on the second floor of a house on one of the main streets. As there was quite a fug in the room I opened one of the windows for ventilation. At once I heard the shuffling of many feet. The whole street was a moving tide of men, women, and children marching in the darkness. Nobody talked; occasionally a woman sobbed. This instinctive method of expressing pent-up feelings was strangely moving. Few in the crowd had not suffered a loss of one kind or another. By comparison our little so-called celebration seemed out of order. The end of the war for the British terminated four long years of regimentation, deprivation, and sacrifice, a sobering thought that persuaded me to leave the party to return to the ship, there to pour out my feelings to Sally in a long letter.

The next morning I was summoned to the office and was told to prepare to leave my ship to command Unit 6, relieving Ashley Adams. This was a blow to the solar plexus to which I had hardly adjusted when a second summons reported the staggering news that all orders were temporarily cancelled pending receipt of details to support a telephone message from Admiral Sims that all Plymouth-based chasers were to start for home as soon as they could be made ready.

Avid discussions among the chaser officers were in agreement that this was no rumor, but we were divided on when a start could be made. There seemed to be only two alternatives, to remain in Plymouth until the North Atlantic weather changed in April, returning by the same route by which we arrived, or start at once and make a run for it to get far enough south along the coast of Africa to catch the northeast trades and summer weather to the West Indies.

Chapter 10

Plymouth to Brest — Pilot Duty

ON NOVEMBER 22, Unit 1 with three other units departed Plymouth for Brest for pilot duty in French ports as assigned. We no longer had unit identification, but *No.'s 177* and *143*, happily still together, were assigned with three others to Brest. Two boats were transferred to St. Nazaire, two to LaPallice, two to the Gironde River (Bordeaux), and two to L'Orient. At least we were one step nearer home.

Before we left Plymouth, Captain Cotton, who had relieved Admiral Bristol, told me that the French were most anxious to buy these chasers and there was little doubt in his mind that a deal would go through. If so, about the middle of January each boat would be taken over by the French and its crew immediately returned to the States. He said that the squadron at Corfu was to proceed to the Philippines!

The Rade de Brest, which had previously seemed full of ships, was crowded beyond belief. My orders directed me to report for duty as harbor pilot to the port director, a pleasant, unruffled captain, United States Coast Guard. On one wall of his office on the second floor of his pier in the Port du Commerce was a blown-up chart of the harbor marked off in squares, each designated by a letter and a number. Most of them bore a tab with the name of a ship.

He explained that every ship on arrival was assigned a square. It was the pilot's duty to board the ship to see that it anchored at its designated square, otherwise with some three hundred ships in the harbor it would take a week for the Port Office to find it.

He looked out the window and grinned. "Here's your first job. See that collier anchored in the entrance to the port, blocking traffic? She knows better, because she is one of a fleet that has been coming in every three weeks or so for the last year with coal from Cardiff under England's contract to supply France with two million tons a month. Her name is *Warfish*, 9,000 tons, and her assigned square is L-16, of which she is perfectly well aware. This is a ploy to get attention, otherwise he might be anchored for a week before we got round to discharging his cargo. That's why he didn't wait for a pilot. Like the rest of us, he wants to get home. Get him the hell out of there, then drop his papers here."

This was my first boarding. *Warfish* was so deep laden that when Connolly laid *No. 143* neatly alongside I had no difficulty in swinging myself up onto her rail where I perched while a red-faced middle-aged man came forward to meet me. He wore dirty blue trousers, a once white turtle neck sweater, and an officer's cap with grease-stained white cap cover and a badge that identified him as the engineer officer.

"Good morning," I said. "Can I see the captain?"

"Oh, aye," he replied in a broad Scot burr. "But he can no see you." I noticed that he was weaving a bit.

"What's your name, sir?"

"McIntosh. What's yours?"

"Moffat," I said.

"That's a guid Scottish name. What's the raist of it?"

"They call me Sandy."

He moved closer. At three feet his breath was overpowering. While I still perched on the rail he wagged a finger and launched into a fascinating statement that I did not attempt to interrupt.

"When a baby in Scotland is chrustened Alexander, while he's a wee one he's called Sandy. When he gets to be one of the lads he's called Alec. Then when he reaches the age of twenty-one, man's estate, it's determined by the community in which he lives whether he is going to be a pillar of the community or a bar fly. If he is going to be a pillar of the community he becomes Alexander. If he is going to be a bar fly he reverts to the Sandy. So you come along now. Ye shall see the captain."

Parenthetically, three weeks later when *Warfish* returned and once more blocked the entrance, I was again sent to get her out of there, and again Mr. McIntosh was the only man on deck. I greeted him with, "How are you, Mac?" He replied solemnly, "Good morning, Alec." I felt there was still hope.

As he had said, the Captain indeed could not see me. He was passed out cold in his bunk, as was the mate whom we looked in on.

"Mr. McIntosh," I said, "this ship must be moved — now. Who's going to do it?"

"We'll move her never fear. There's plenty of steam up. I'll go on the forecastle and get the anchor under foot. Then I'll nip down to the engine room and whustle up the voice tube. Then you can give me bells and put the old whoor where you want. When you ring 'through with engines' I'll nip back up to the forecastle and let go the bloody anchor, and there you are."

And so two of us moved a 9,000-ton steamer safely to L-16.

I waved to *No. 143* to take me off. Mr. McIntosh saw me to the rail, producing a large envelope from an inside pocket.

"Ye'll be taking our papers ashore, then? The Captain will thank ye kindly." Then he added confidentially, "It means we get home a week sooner."

Our duty time was spent alongside the dock standing by the telephone for orders to make jaunts to ships at anchor or to board new arrivals in the *goulet*, or outer entrance to the harbor. The duty seldom took us outside. Finding the right square in fog when range marks ashore were not visible meant memorizing what ships were already located in the vicinity of the destination. Ships were not moved at night if avoidable, and never if visibility was less than a quarter mile.

My first night boarding was typical of many. The telephoned orders were, "Find *Santa Anna*. Make regular boarding visit. Anchor in G-12." I had quite a time finding her as she had already entered and anchored at random.

We prowled around with the searchlight throwing into relief tiers upon tiers of decks towering far above us. The sound of our exhausts echoed in the night from the steel sides of ships that showed in the circle of light garish splotches of camouflage, ever changing in color as we glided through blackness to the next one. Then for a space we would lose the warm smells of cooking, rubber matting, and steam to breathe the fragrant salt of the ocean.

To do justice to this boarding job one should be able to speak fluently and profanely in Norwegian, Danish, Swedish, Italian, Greek, French, Spanish, and Cockney. They were all here. At night when you got an unintelligible jargon in reply to a hail, it was necessary to run around under the stern and throw the searchlight on the name and port of hail to see whether the bird was calling you names or whether he really was *Ida Maru* spoken in Japanese.

After half an hour we found *Santa Anna*, a great passenger and freight ship belonging to W. R. Grace & Company. As we came up to that lofty wall, with its threadlike Jacob's ladder dangling from the great white way of her promenade deck, we felt smaller than the lifeboats above our mast.

I climbed five decks up the ladder, boarding book in teeth in real pilot style, into a new world, while *No. 143*'s red and green eyes far below receded into the night to the clatter of exhausts as she backed away to stand by. For the first time I think I realized how small a chaser really was, and was momentarily awed at the thought that we really had crossed the Atlantic in that one.

Met at the rail by the fourth mate, I was conducted for what seemed a mile along a brilliantly lighted deck, spacious and empty as a street at midnight. Up two flights of steps we stepped through a door over a high sill, and found ourselves in the presence of the chief mate. The room, fore and aft, measured a good twenty-five feet and almost as wide. Around one corner ran a deep, red leather settee, on which lounged a couple of Army officers, Quartermaster Corps, supercargos. The mate sat in a swivel chair, his feet on an enormous flat topped desk. This was going to sea!

Directing the quartermaster to square G-12 under the watchful eye of the chief mate was easy. It was not far. *Santa Anna* was the biggest ship I had controlled.

Returning to the surface of the sea, where I lived, after all that white enamel and dazzling light I saw *No. 143* as she really was, worn, battered, and indescribably cramped, but she was home, in a sense, and cozy.

Since arrival at Brest I had explored every possible means of getting detached and sent home. Even if orders were forthcoming, obtaining passage to the States seemed impossible because of Army brass priorities on every crammed transport. We learned that the chasers, all except the five at Brest had already started south. Rumor had it that the Brest boats, if unsold, were to stay until all United

States troops had left France. At this time the French had agreed to buy only *No. 177*, but did not say when delivery was to be made. George was on tenterhooks.

Finally I evolved a brilliant scheme that just possibly might bear fruit. I suggested to Captain Diotte how expensive, uncomfortable, crowded, and detrimental to morale it was to maintain a full complement of two officers and twenty-four men aboard the chasers on present duty. He directed me to submit in writing a recommendation to reduce complement to one officer and fifteen men, which would receive his favorable endorsement, a first step in proceeding through channels.

These channels proved to be tortuous and time-consuming. A flag office and a district office were each under command of a rear admiral. The chasers came under the operating orders of the latter and the personnel jurisdiction of the former. For his protection from the petty details of life, each admiral had a sizable staff to winnow papers for him, as well as an aide who was a final barrier to reaching his presence.

The letter I concocted was a masterpiece of brevity and logic. With Captain Diotte's guidance the routing was properly indicated. A paragraph at the end requested briefly that immediate transportation be provided "in accordance with the above." Beneath this I had typed, "Approved . . . . Rear Admiral, USN". So, on this 20th day of December the letter, for better or worse, was launched in the uncertain waters of the guard mail.

Occasionally orders from the port office were unusual. One day *No. 177* had the duty and I, having nothing else to do, went along with George for the ride.

"Find small unidentified tug towing barge. Obtain name, port of origin and mission."

We found her steaming slowly close to the beach and came within hail. She flew the United States flag, a small gray, harbor-type tug carrying on her funnel the insignia of the Army Transport Service. The skipper was a young warrant officer with a crew of six enlisted men. The barge was coal-laden, deep in the water.

It took time for his information to penetrate, that he had just arrived from New York, towing the barge the whole way, refueling from his cargo when weather permitted. As the barge was leaking badly the skipper was seeking a spot along the shore where he could beach it before it sank. We escorted his tow to a shallow cove, well up the harbor, then escorted the tug to the port director's pier to report and replenish. This outfit must have been dispatched by some officer with spurs on his desk who had no conception of the suicidal nature of such a trip at this season. An Army blunder saved by a fine performance of seamanship! When we bade the skipper goodbye he said he was not going to worry about the future until he had hit the sack for about twelve hours.

An ever-increasing hazard to small craft flying the United States flag in moving around the harbor was avoiding collision with the little bluff-bowed French fishing boats. They sailed surprisingly fast with their patched red sails and were expertly maneuvered in traffic by their piratical-looking Breton crews. A new game was born when the fishermen discovered that if they could contrive a minor collision they could file a claim for damage at the office of the port director where they could collect demurrage for every day, or fraction of a day, they were there. As it sometimes took this busy office a few days to handle the paper work and reach a decision, even if the claim was dismissed demurrage was far more profitable than fishing. Frequently the chasers were called on for some nimble evasion to avoid a fisherman lurking in ambush behind a big ship at anchor.

By December 24 my fateful letter had not been returned disapproved by any of the channels of endorsement. I decided that therefore it must have reached the admiral's office by this time where it was probably buried deep in some basket. I decided to call on the admiral's aide.

Fortunately the aide was in good humor, possibly because of the Christmas spirit in the air. He appeared to have some time on his hands and dug up my letter, which was just where I thought it would be. He agreed to lay it before the admiral. The great man was visible through the door of the inner office, moodily staring at the rain beating against the windows. He, too, seemed to have time on his hands.

"Now?" I suggested.

The aide took a look at his idle boss. "All right," he said.

The admiral inspected the letter as it was placed before him. "What's this about?" he asked casually.

"The chasers have too many men aboard for present duty and request a reduction in complement, sir," he replied succinctly.

The admiral ran his eye over the first paragraph. He flipped the page, even as he reached for a pen. The aide returned with the precious document in his hand, signed.

"Much obliged," I said casually. "This will make things much easier. And Merry Christmas to you!"

The officer who handled transportation of personnel was a harassed two-striper. After waiting in line for forty minutes my turn came. My heart was pounding.

I knew that the United States Hospital Ship *Henderson* was sailing for New York.

"Sir, I want transportation on USS *Henderson* for four officers and forty men."

The lieutenant promptly blew up. Among others on the waiting list he had two hundred Army officers of the rank of captain or higher in excess of the accommodations available and he would be damned if he knew by what authority an ensign came in demanding immediate transportation, anyhow. "You'll be lucky," he added, "if you get home within four months."

With pardonable pride I handed him the letter, pointing silently to the word "immediate" and to the signature under the magic word "approved".

He read the letter and stared at me. "If you put this across you rate going home. It's murder," he said and laughed.

The activity of the next three hours defied description, but within that period the other three officers and forty men, their records completed and pay accounts transferred were aboard the *Henderson* with orders for home.

At 1600 hours I had completed my own records, signed the log for the last time, and turned the command over to Connolly. Lines were cast off, and in five minutes we were alongside the ship that was to take me home to Sally and the children. It was the first moment I had had to let the realization sink in, so that it was with difficulty that I spoke to the officer of the deck who sauntered up to return my salute. Probably every officer who came over the rail asked the same question, "When do we sail?"

"If repairs are completed, 2300 tonight."

Chapter 11

Home

AT 2000 HOURS there was a knock on the door of the cabin I was to share with an Army major who had not yet appeared. An orderly stood in the passage.

"Executive officer wishes you to report to him at once, sir."

Lightheartedly I slipped into my tunic and followed the man to the main deck. I stepped over a high threshold and found myself in a turmoil of clattering typewriters. At the end of the compartment a commander was signing papers.

"You sent for me, sir," I said, giving my name.

"There is a running boat leaving in twenty minutes," he said briefly and handed me a signal slip addressed to me.

In the language of the Navy it directed me to report at 2100 hours to the port director on charges arising from collision.

"Don't you know you can't run away from these things?" snapped the executive officer. "If you did get away with it you would be returned to Brest on your arrival in New York. Get your baggage and shove off."

There was nothing to say.

Pushing my way among the happy homeward-bound troops on the main deck, back to the cabin which I was not to occupy, I packed my gear and tried to think.

The running boat was popping at the gangway when I requested permission to leave the ship. The rain drizzled as though it had never stopped. It seemed that the cavernous motor sailer in which I was the lone passenger was a fitting tomb under its dark canopy. A megaphone bellowed; I heard the tinkle of a bell and the coxswain's remarks to the bow man as he languidly pushed his foot against the tiller. The boat gathered way. Under a swinging light bulb the machinist's mate crouched like a goblin over his engine; aft the widespread legs of the coxswain showed like a shadowy part of the craft against the black night.

After an eternity the boat bumped the landing float. The stairs up to the Port Office were endless this night. My steps echoed loudly on the narrow stairway to the silent offices. A sleepy orderly sat at the door of the director's office. The room was empty.

Hastily I searched the director's basket for guard mail. Buried in the bottom of the tray was my report, the seal unbroken. For fifteen minutes I sat and listened to the ticking of the clock until it became confused with the beating of my heart, and I had a silly lump in my throat. The downstairs door banged. Heavy footsteps sounded on the stairs. Somehow they did not seem to ring with authority. Once they stumbled. Presently in the doorway appeared the stocky figure of the new lieutenant commander detailed that very day to assist the director. On his face, red perhaps from years at sea, was a stern look of concentration on the matter in hand, which was divesting himself of his rain coat.

I stood at attention awaiting the first salvo.

It started with a description of the enormity of my offense, interspersed with allusions to regulations; it proceeded with a tribute to the greatness of the United States Navy. From that point it touched the heartstrings with a pitiful picture of the poor French fisherman returning from his day's toil to be wantonly run down by a reserve, wantonly, sir, and deliberately. Thence it wound up in a review of the facts, to which was appended the most flowery, the most outrageous, the most impossible peroration that ever graced an after-dinner speech.

Quite overcome with his exertions he sank into a chair. Figuratively I appraised his steam pressure as zero.

"Commander," I said with a pleasant smile, "I've got an earful for you, too. May I shoot?"

The appraisal was correct. He grinned, his own words still warming his heart.

"At 1002 this morning, while returning from the duty trip," I began, "at a moment when my vessel was drifting with engines stopped and no way on, I was run down by this fisherman, wantonly, sir, and deliberately!"

He stared suspiciously, but let it pass.

"Furthermore," I continued, "every requirement provided by regulations was at once complied with in my detailed report, now in the basket in front of you, which owing to the incredibly rotten guard mail system in this port, did not reach you in time to prevent my being placed unfairly in a position entirely incompatible with my record. Please read the report, or perhaps you will allow me to read it to you."

He listened attentively to the brief outline of facts.

"And that frog swine trying to hold us for demurrage!" he blurted.

"Yes," I said. "He knows he can't collect any claim when the facts are known, so he puts a value on the services of his boat of four times what it ever earned, which he will collect for each day or fraction of a day from the time he ran into us until his claim is dismissed. That's the law."

"One day is all that bird will collect," he said grimly. "Orderly, go get that fish-eating, low-down dirty frog in the other office, and the interpreter."

A door opened down the corridor, emitting an incessant monologue of atrocious Cape Breton which moved toward us, oblivious to the interpreter's admonition of *"Tais toi, vieux cochon!"*

The stream of conversation was directed, forthwith at the commander.

"What does he say?" he demanded of the interpreter. The old fisherman, a filthy specimen with a bad eye, repeated his plaint with flying hands, glaring at me the while.

"Silence!" thundered the commander. "Hold his arms!"

This form of silence was applied effectively and joyfully by the interpreter and orderly, both stalwart gobs, and the interpreter told the story that had brought me ashore, adding at the end, "I believe he's lying, sir."

"I know damn well he is," said the commander. "Tell him he ran into a vessel of the United States Navy deliberately to get demurrage money. Tell him he's lucky not to be in jail. Tell him if he doesn't get the hell out of here in thirty seconds he will be. And if he doesn't step lively help him down the stairs."

Down the stairs he went, still talking, ably assisted on his way. The commander and I were alone.

"My ship sails in an hour, sir," I said hopefully. "Am I free to go — home?"

"You are," he said, "and a Merry Christmas to you. Will you join me on my way uptown?"

"I'll accept the thought for the deed, sir, if you'll take an extra one for me," I replied.

"I'll do that little thing," he said, rising. "Orderly, telephone the director's barge to come to the float immediately to take an officer off to the *Henderson*."

At the head of the steps to the float we parted. If he had kissed me, I would have kissed him back.

That last swift dash in the director's barge, with each wave tossed aside leaving the city of Brest astern, was a glorious experience.

As I stepped to the *Henderson*'s gangway, the coxswain said, "Shall I wait for you, sir?"

"If you do, you'll wait a long time, Jack; I'm going home!"

On reporting for pilot duty at Brest, I had been designated officer-in-charge of the chasers operating in that port, which must have been a mistake because George was senior to me. Consequently it was I who had submitted the names of the four officers and forty men attached to my letter and now approved by the admiral for immediate transfer to the United States. The list of course included George, the only other married officer in the unit, and all sixteen of the married enlisted men.

The *Henderson* sailed on schedule at 2300 hours on Christmas Eve. I introduced myself to my affable cabin mate, a Major Glore, and turned in, too excited to sleep. Thoughts of Sally waiting, as eager as I to be in each other's arms, made the voyage ahead seem interminable.

The first day out from Brest the *Henderson*, an elderly twin-screw steamship with a normal speed of fifteen knots, lost a propeller blade. Even at speed reduced to ten knots the vibration was appalling. This meant that if not further reduced by adverse weather our arrival in New York would be January 3. This four days delay seemed, at the moment, out of all proportion heartbreaking.

Otherwise the passage was uneventful, subchaser weather all

the way; nothing to do but sleep, dream of home, conform to shipboard routine, and yearn for the end to regimented life.

At first daylight on January 3, I showered, shaved, and donned my last clean linen. My weather-worn uniform and cap looked shabby. The insignia was salt-tarnished, but the brass buttons and the shoes were painstakingly polished. After packing, I went on deck.

The day was still, gray, and bitter cold. The *Henderson* nosed slowly up New York harbor toward the ramparts of Manhattan to her pier on the Hoboken side of the Hudson River, to be taken in charge for berthing by six fussing tugs.

Family letters had kept me informed about my two brothers. Bob was still in France, now transferred from his unpleasant detail in Bordeaux to man the information booth at a rail center outside Paris. Don, also bilingual, in 1916 had joined the American Field Service in France as an ambulance driver. When the United States entered the war, he resigned to enter an Army officers training program at Plattsburgh, New York, for reserves.

He graduated with the rank of captain. He fully expected his experience at the front would take him back to France, but the Army squandered his talents by ordering him to duty on the docks of Hoboken as embarkation officer.

He had recently married Sally's youngest sister, whom he had met when she was eleven, the year Sally and I were married. Don, at the time, was a freshman at Harvard, and he told us then that he had decided to wait for her. To the delight of both families, when she was eighteen the marriage came to pass.

Don had received word that I was arriving on the *Henderson*. I hoped his duties would permit him to meet the ship so that he could steer me to Sally who would, I supposed, be held behind some sort of barrier until the passengers had cleared customs. My footlocker and sea-bag were already on deck near the gangway.

The ship moved silently and slowly forward along the wall of the pier shed. Briefcase under my arm, I bulldozed my way to the rail. On the stringpiece near an opening where a gangway hung suspended I spotted my handsome, blonde brother in his Army greatcoat. As we drew abeam he saw me. With a broad smile he jerked his thumb over his shoulder. I relaxed. He knew where Sally was.

At the foot of the gangway we shook hands. "She is waiting for

Alexander W. Moffat, Captain, USNR (Ret.), 1946,
from a painting by Sally

you in my office where it's warm. Come along," he said, grinning.

"How's Polly? Haven't had a chance to write since I heard the wonderful news. You know how I've always loved that child. Congratulations!"

"She's just fine. Sends her love." We could see our breaths in the arctic temperature of the cavernous, dimly lighted pier, echoing to the noise of freight handling.

We headed toward a partitioned corner housing customs and Army offices. "Through that door. You'll find my cubicle marked 'Embarkation Officer.' She is in there waiting for you. I've sent the clerk away. After the baggage has been distributed I'll come back for you with my pet customs officer. God bless! I know how you must feel." He was gone.

My heart was thumping when I opened the glazed door to a small, warm office. Then she was in my arms, a lithe little figure in a silver-gray fur coat and cap, a bright red silk scarf at her throat. She buried her head in my shoulder. Neither of us could speak. Then she leaned back and took my face between her hands, eyes bright with tears, lips parted in a smile that was for me alone.

My own eyes were wet. I said shakily, "Isn't there something in this damned office you can stand on so I can kiss you properly?" Our faces were a foot apart.

"It'll keep, my darling. Right now I just want to feast my eyes. You always were too big. We'll be home in no time."

We sat snuggled together on the edge of Don's desk while she answered my questions about the children.

Don returned with a smiling customs man. At the letter M my possessions were passed and chalked without opening. A porter with a push truck was summoned from thin air. Don had parked Sally's little gray Willys-Overland touring car with the wire wheels inside the barrier that held back the public. After we had loaded my gear in the back seat and rebuttoned the side curtains, Don thoughtfully started the engine so that the hot air heater could function while we returned to his office to fetch Sally. She elected to drive. At 7:30 we left the pier. Don well understood my gratitude at thus being whisked through the formalities.

On the ride home words between us trickled only intermittently over the dam of our pent-up emotions, but each of us was comfortingly aware of the proximity of the other.

Finally we entered our little tree-lined, dead-end street overlooking the Flushing meadows and turned into our two-story white house set in a patch of lawn fronted by a picket fence. The short driveway to the garage passed the front door, which was on the side of the house. There we stopped, our arrival announced by frantic welcoming barks inside. Nothing was changed.

By the time we opened the front door we were met by an ecstatic bull terrier, a little blonde girl hopping up and down shouting, "Daddy! Daddy! Daddy!" and Lizzie Burke mopping tears with her apron. I sat down on the stairs so Mari could fling her arms around my neck and I could hug her.

Peeping shyly behind Lizzie's skirts was two-year-old Sissie, whom I had not seen since she was a nursing baby. She was a sturdy child with dark ringlets, dark eyes, and flaming red cheeks. She stared at me curiously, then said, "Why, you are my daddy," but took no chances on approaching closer. Both little girls wore bibs.

Sally said, "He's your very own daddy, all right. Now you both go with Lizzie and finish your breakfast. We'll all visit later. You're a good girl, Sissie, you haven't spilled on your bib."

"No," she replied solemnly, "this is a *good* bib." Lizzie retired, sobbing, followed by the children and the dog. He never missed a handout.

Our bedroom door closed behind us. The cheerful, warm room was just as I remembered it, smelling faintly and tantalizingly of woman — my woman. No word was spoken between us.

At long last we were again one body, and then one soul.

Reluctantly, drowsily we returned to earth.

Fervently I said, "Thank you!"

"Thank *you!*"

"I smell bacon cooking."

Abruptly she sat up, fussing with her hair, "Oh, you poor dear, I forgot all about breakfast. You must be famished — and you are so thin!"

Home.

Postscripts

DURING THE WAR 105 subchasers on both sides of the Atlantic were engaged in operating against enemy submarines. The Bureau of Navigation, which kept account of the value of all allied shipping sunk by enemy submarines, entered a credit of $20,000,000 for each submarine known to have been destroyed. The destruction of two enemy submarines was credited to the subchaser account. Thus, in value of merchant tonnage saved, $40,000,000 more than offset the cost of building and operating those 105 subchasers for the duration of the war. To which chasers these two kills were credited, we never learned.

The effective strength of the enemy was never underestimated by the high command. While on duty in the English Channel, Unit 1 twice had the rare opportunity to attack an enemy submarine. The submarine attacked on May 30, 1918, had surfaced close aboard *No. 143*. I am personally convinced that it could not have survived the first and the subsequent accurate depth charging to which it was subjected by *No.'s 177* and *143*, then operating as a two-boat unit. We could not be officially credited with a kill because we were unable to produce any tangible evidence, nor was there present a senior officer of the United States Navy witness to the engagement.

Unofficial information later reached us through friends in British operations that a German submarine identified by number was known to have been operating in the area at the time of our attack. British Intelligence in Germany reported that this submarine had never returned to port.

A promotion to lieutenant (JG) effective September 19, 1918, did not reach me until January 5, 1919, on which date I was sworn in. The pay, however, was retroactive.

The following longhand letter dated December 12, 1919, was received from Captain Lyman A. Cotten, USN, who had succeeded Rear Admiral Mark Bristol, USN, as commanding officer of United States Naval Base 27 at Plymouth, England

DEPARTMENT OF THE NAVY

General Board
Washington

My dear Moffat,

Please accept my best congratulations upon receiving the "distinguished service cross." It is a belated but well-deserved recognition of your war services. I hope it will help in keeping fresh memories of subchaser days.

If you are in Washington any time be sure and look me up. Will always be glad to see you.

Very sincerely yours,
L. A. Cotten

Another letter dated November 11, 1920 reads as follows:

THE SECRETARY OF THE NAVY

Washington

SIR:-

The President of the United States takes pleasure in presenting the NAVY CROSS to

LIEUTENANT (JG) ALEXANDER W. MOFFAT, USNRF

for services during the World War as set forth in the following:

Citation:
"For distinguished service in the line of his profession as

Commanding Officer of the USSC #*143*, engaged in the important, exacting and hazardous duty of patrolling the waters of the war zone and operating against enemy submarines."

For the President.

Josephus Daniels
Secretary of the Navy

Appendix

VITAL STATISTICS, World War I Subchasers, United States Navy

Construction:
    Wood, compartmented with seven steel bulkheads

Dimensions:

Length over all	110′
Length water line	105′
Extreme beam over guards	15′ 5″
Beam on deck	14′ 9″
Draft to bottom of deadwood	5′ 11″
Full load displacement	75 Tons

Propulsion:
    Triple propellers 39″ diameter x 57 ½″ pitch

    Three six-cylinder gasoline engines rated 220 h.p. at 500 rpm, bore 10″ stroke 11″ directly connected to propeller shafts, compressed air starting and reversing. Cylinders individually cast, mounted on open base crankcase. Ignition Bosch waterproof magnetic spark plugs with low tension wiring.

Fuel Capacity:
    Total 2,500 gallons carried in four tanks shaped to hull in compartment forward of forward engine room bulkhead beneath the floor of the officers' quarters.

Speed:

Operating on one engine at 350 rpm cruising speed of 8 knots yielded maximum radius of 1000 nautical miles. Maximum theoretical speed with three engines at 500 rpm of 16 knots was unattainable because hull was loaded 5″ deeper than designed draft. Maximum actual speed on three engines was 12 knots, on two engines 10½ knots, on one engine 9 knots.

Auxiliaries:

One two-cylinder gasoline engine rated 10 hp connected on one end to a 4½ kw generator, on the other end to a combination 3″ bilge and fire pump. Each main engine was connected to an individual air compressor.

All the foregoing machinery was designed and built by Standard Motor Construction Company of New Jersey.

Armament:

One 3″ 23-caliber gun mounted on forward deck.

One Y-gun firing simultaneously two 300-lb. depth charges by a 3″ blank cartridge, mounted amidships aft of engine room house.

Two racks mounted on stern deck, each holding six 300-lb. depth charges.

Two 30-caliber Browning machine guns, one mounted on each wing of bridge.

Magazine:

In compartment between steel bulkheads beneath Y-gun, capable of storing 100 rounds high explosive shells for 3″ gun, 50 rounds 3″ shells for Y-gun, 200 rounds machine-gun cartridges and 12 300 lb. depth charges.

Index